THE PROMISES OF GOD

Inspirational Stress Relieving Designs

THE PROMISES OF GOD
Inspirational Stress Relieving Designs

Published in the United States by When Heaven Speaks, LLC
P.O. Box 55
Pooler, GA 31322
www.whenheavenspeakspublishing.com

Copyright © 2020 TWYLIA G. REID
ISBN: 9798578663390

All rights reserved. No part of this book may be reproduced, distributed, or transmitted in any form by any means, graphic, electronic, or mechanical, including photocopy, recording, taping, or by any information storage or retrieval system, without permission in writing from the publisher, except in the case of reprints in the context of reviews, quotes, or references.

Special discounts are available on bulk quantity purchases by book clubs, associations, and special interest groups. For details, email: info@twyliareid.com or call 912-335-3799.

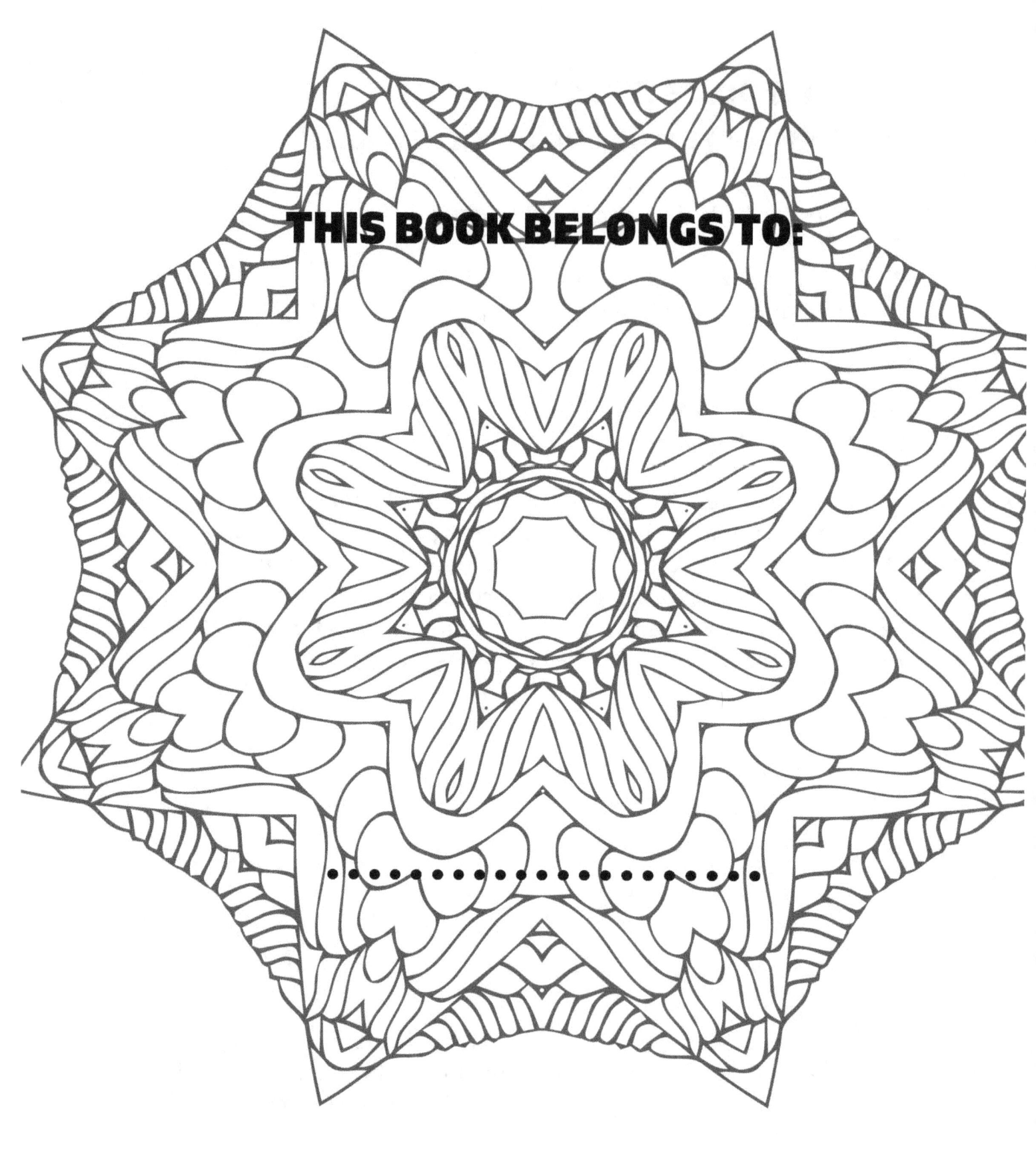

THIS BOOK BELONGS TO:

....

THE PROMISES OF GOD

God's promises are very important. They are the pathways where Christ meets the soul. God's promises are the chief aids to our life and to our daily growth. Whether you realize it or not, God's promises are more useful to us than the air we breathe! Therefore, it's vital we know, and understand that God does not promise to give us everything we want. But, He does promise that, as we pray, He will give us everything we need in order to be fully satisfied in Him. This is awesome news because it allows us to see His promises, trust His promises, and be transformed by His promises!

We live in a sinful world that is filled with conditional promises and relationships. Sometimes even those closest to us let us down. Despite this reality, our greatest need is to be loved unconditionally. God provides us with that as no one else can. When I think about God's unconditional love for me and others and what it looks like I am in total AWE! When our heart is broken, God is there and His heart is broken too. When no one else understands, God does and He sends the Comforter, the Holy Spirit, to help us. When we feel left out, isolated, or rejected, we should remember the wounds on Jesus' hands because those wounds allow Him to understand our pain.

In Matthew 6:9-13, Jesus offers a model prayer. He says to start our prayers with praise, acknowledging God for who He is, where He is, and what He can do. Then we must pray for His will to be done. God promises that His will shall come to pass, but we must be open to His will. Prayer prepares our hearts to carry out His will. Then we will acknowledge and understand it. Jesus also said we can pray for our daily bread...our sustenance to survive, as well as for forgiveness and protection.

Coloring Bible verses is an easy way for us to meditate day and night on the word of God. Coloring can help you relax and reduce stress at the same time. This inspirational coloring book features uplifting quotes and scripture verses for Christians who love to color. This inspirational coloring book is perfect for color enthusiasts of all ages who want to create works of beauty and devotion. These uplifting Scripture quotes and beautiful designs range from simple to complex so that you can spend minutes or hours enjoying a single image. Some days you just need a break. For many, studying calming Bible verses about patience to help you get through the day or powerful Bible verses about courage is a way to find balance in your busy life. But many have discovered another way that combines deep devotional time with art, specifically coloring.

This book features encouraging Scripture quotes of God's promises to us including "God heals the brokenhearted", "I can do all things through Christ who gives me strength", and many more. Designed to give you both peace and inspiration, this adult coloring book lets you focus on the beauty of scripture and bring it to life through coloring.

Imaginative backgrounds, patterns, scenery, and borders provide hours of coloring relaxation for everyone. Each page turn delivers reassuring promises from Scripture and a splendid ink drawing that can be filled with color. THE PROMISES OF GOD will fill your heart and inspire you as the artwork draws you in. Coloring is meditative and quiets and calms the restless spirit.

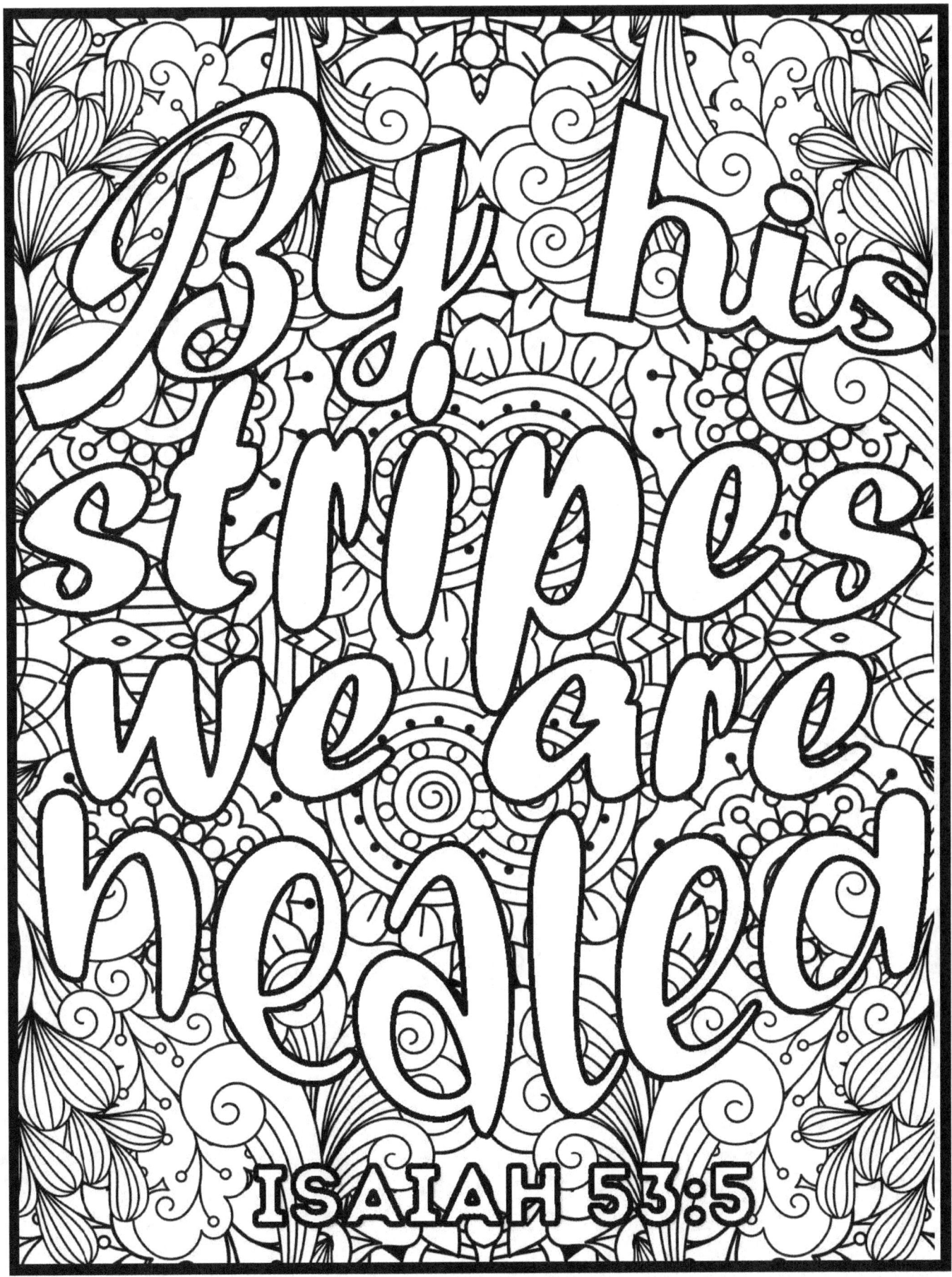

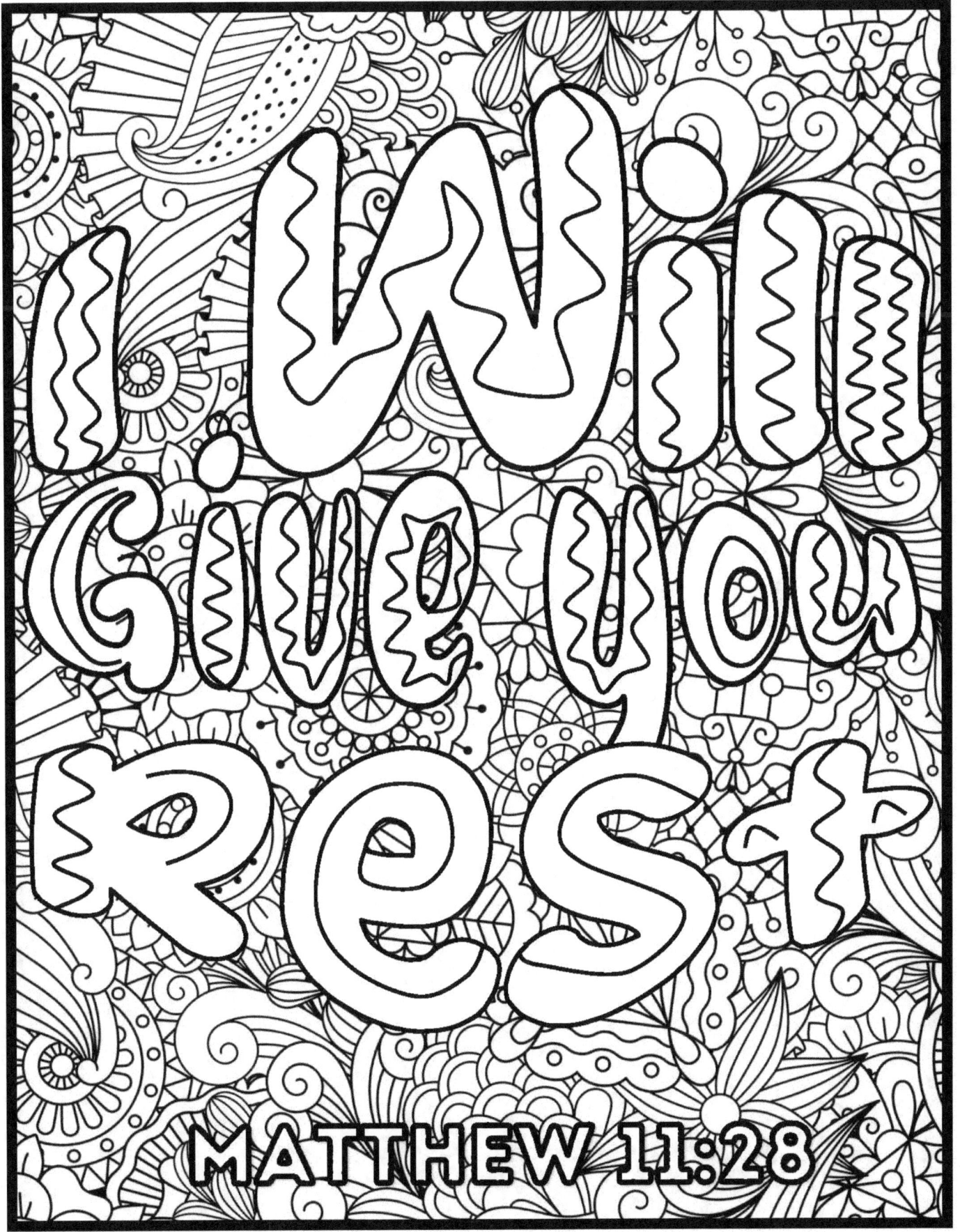

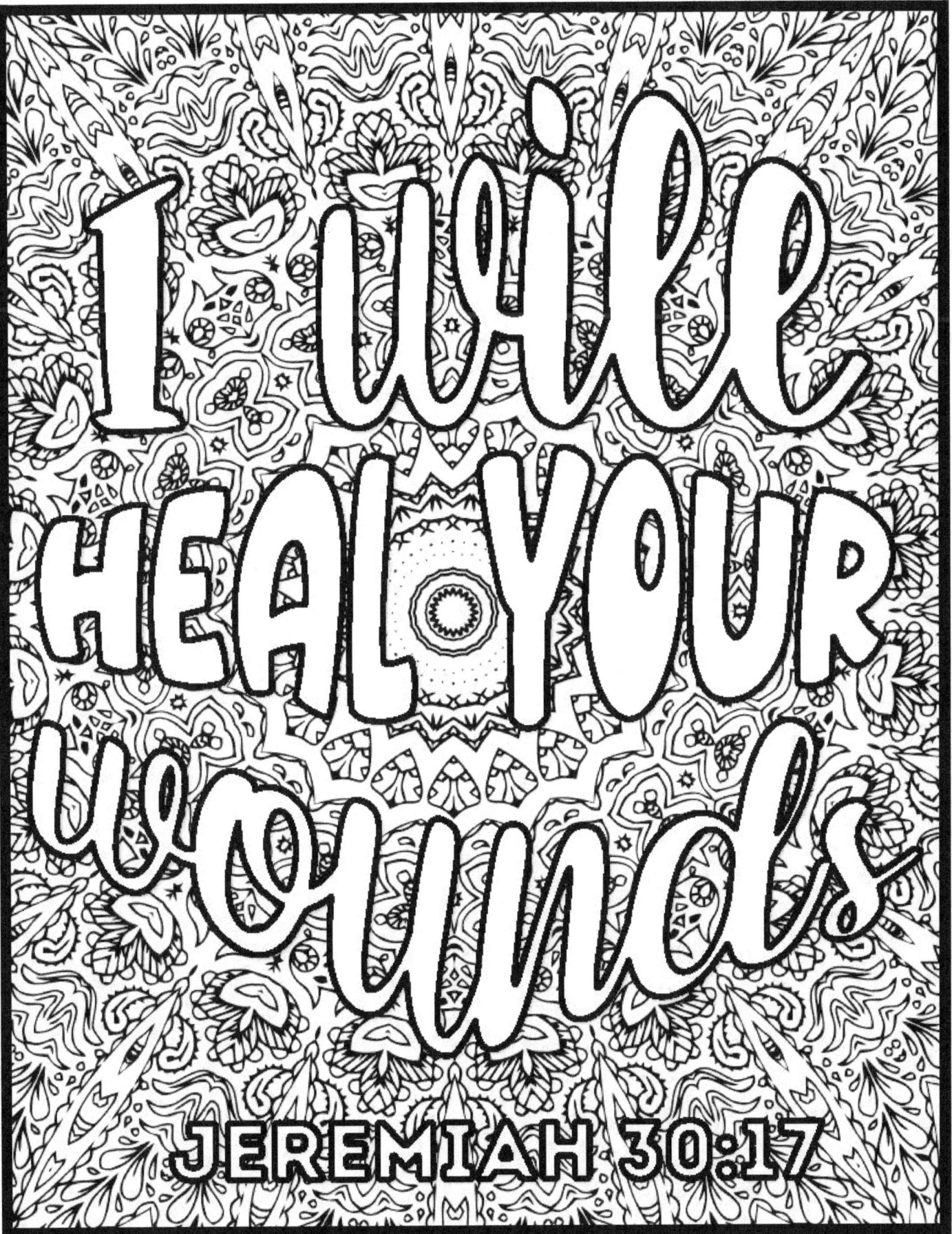

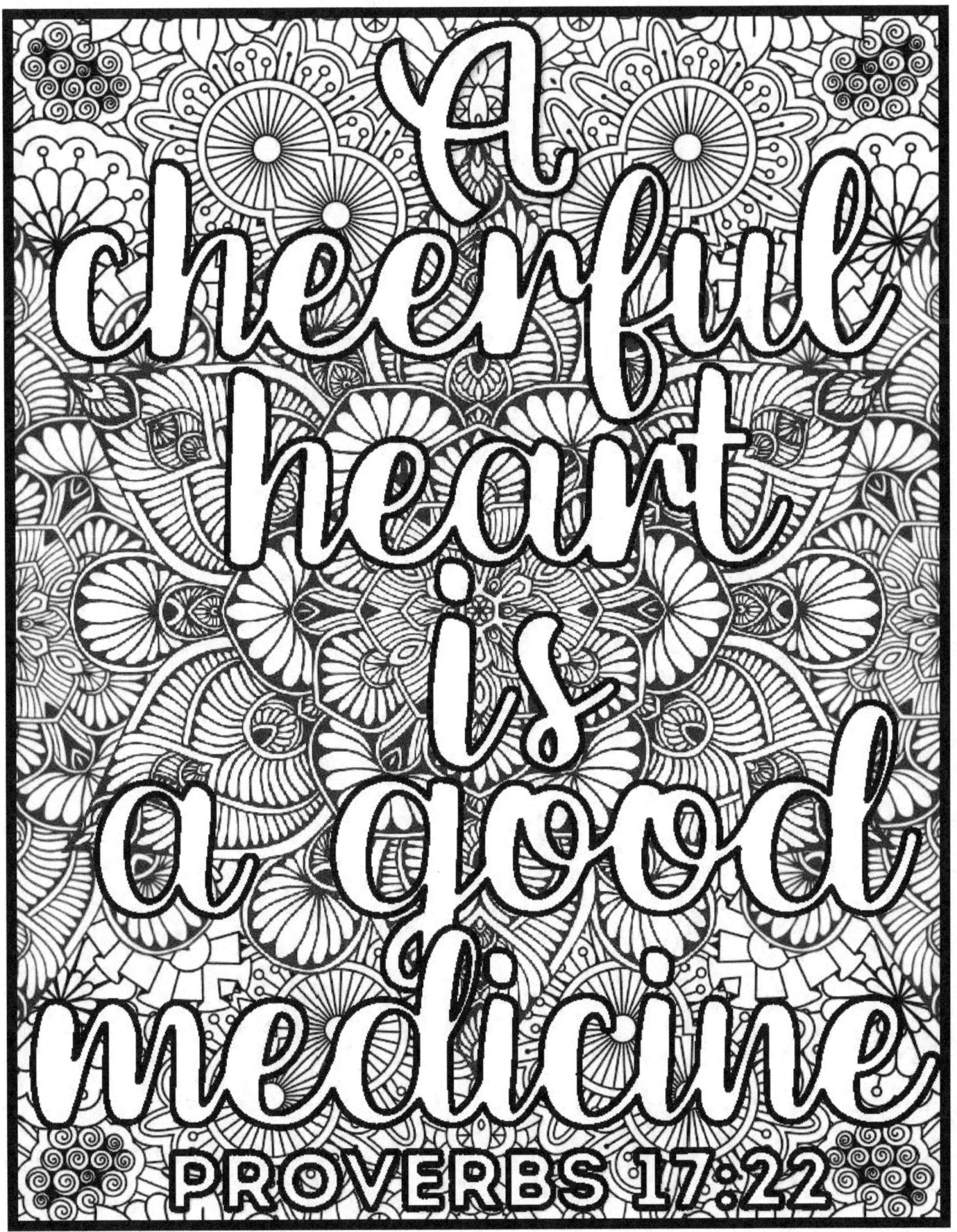

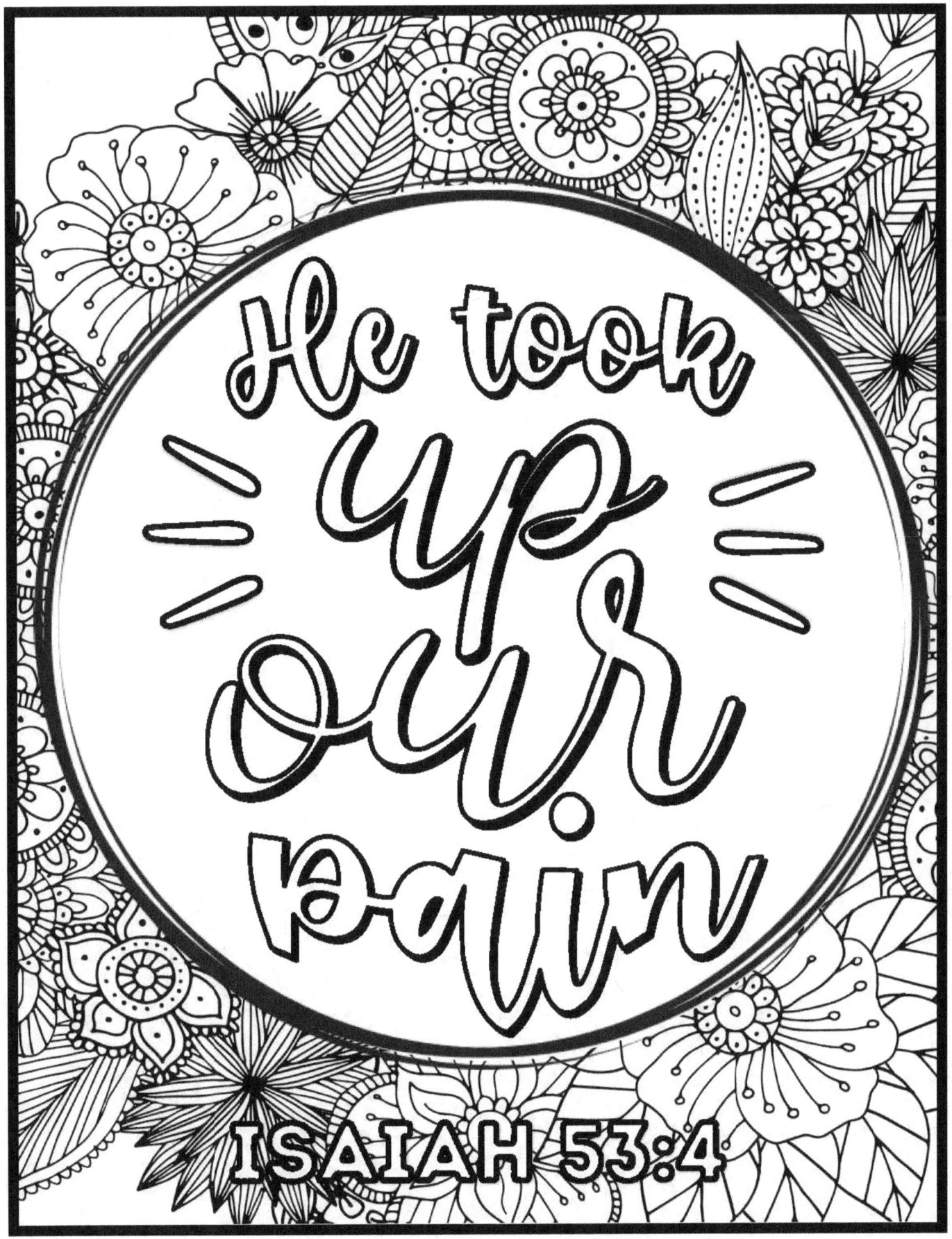

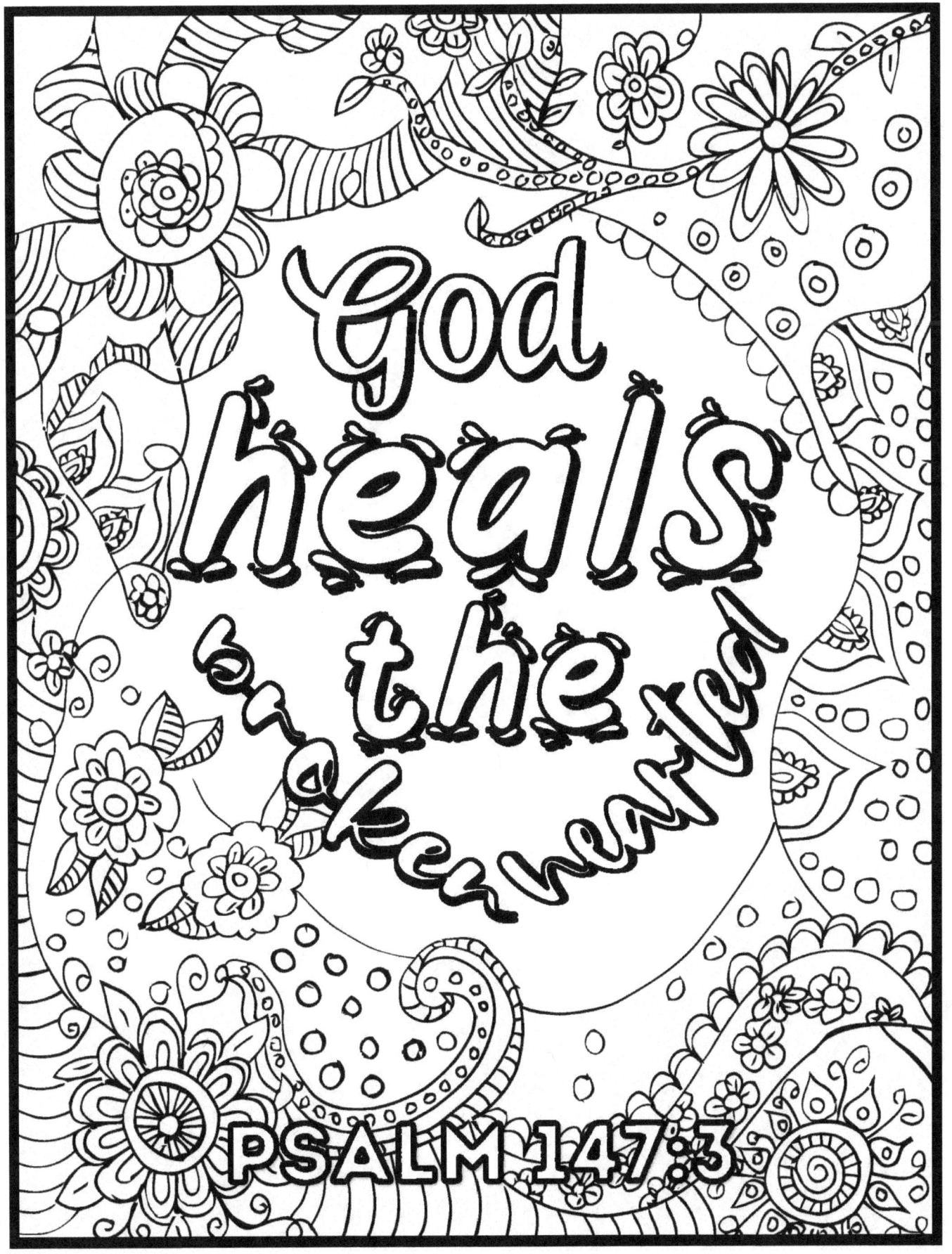

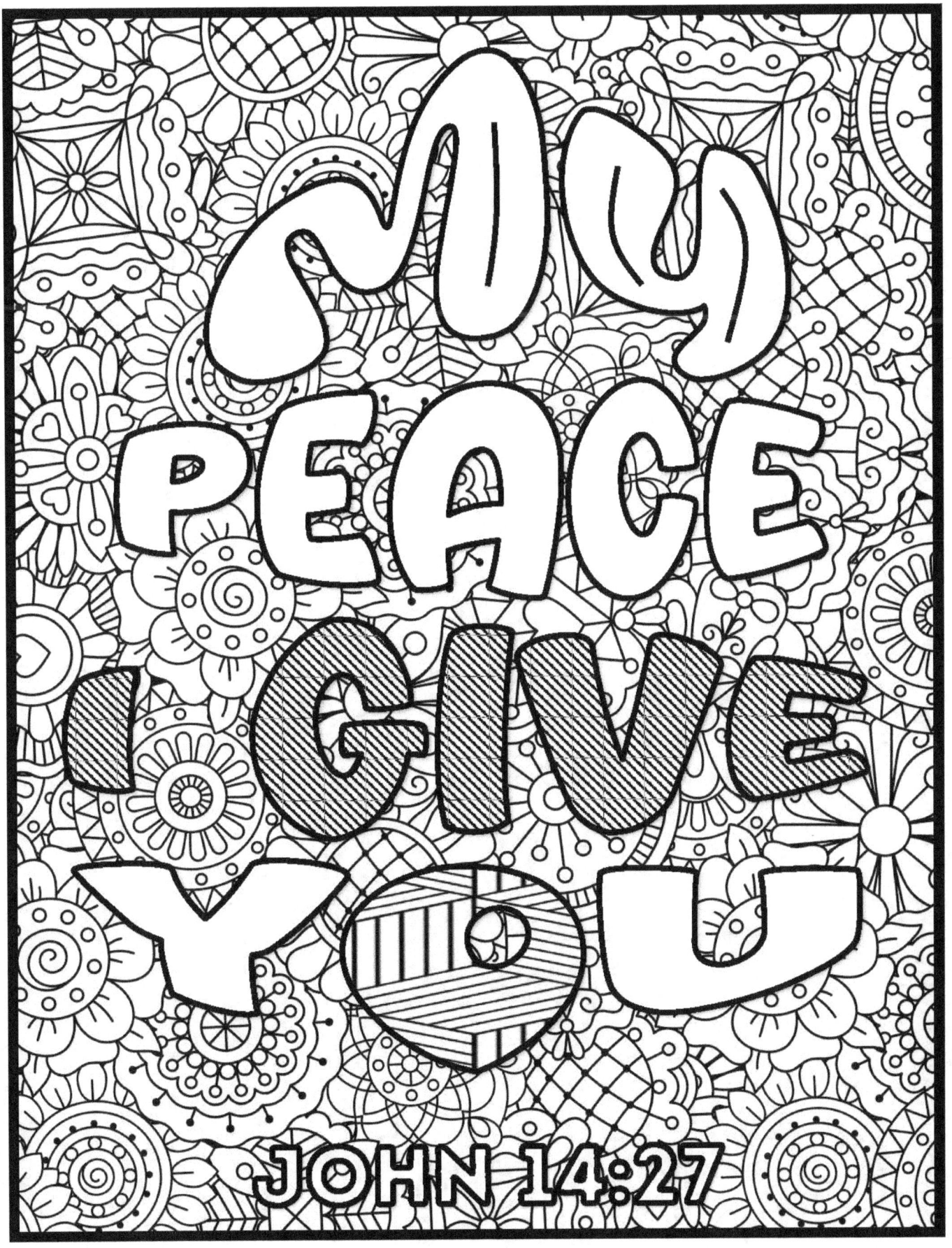

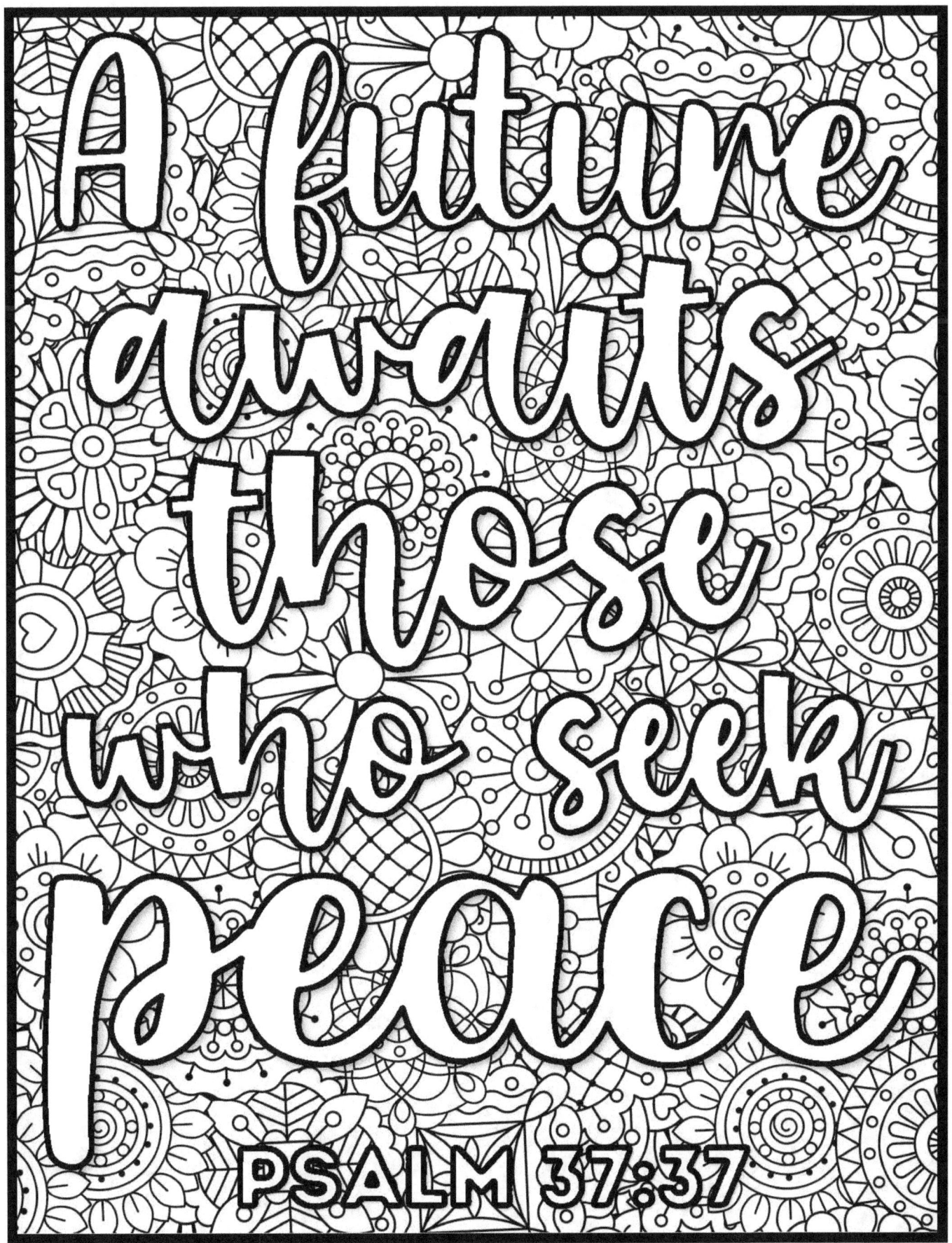

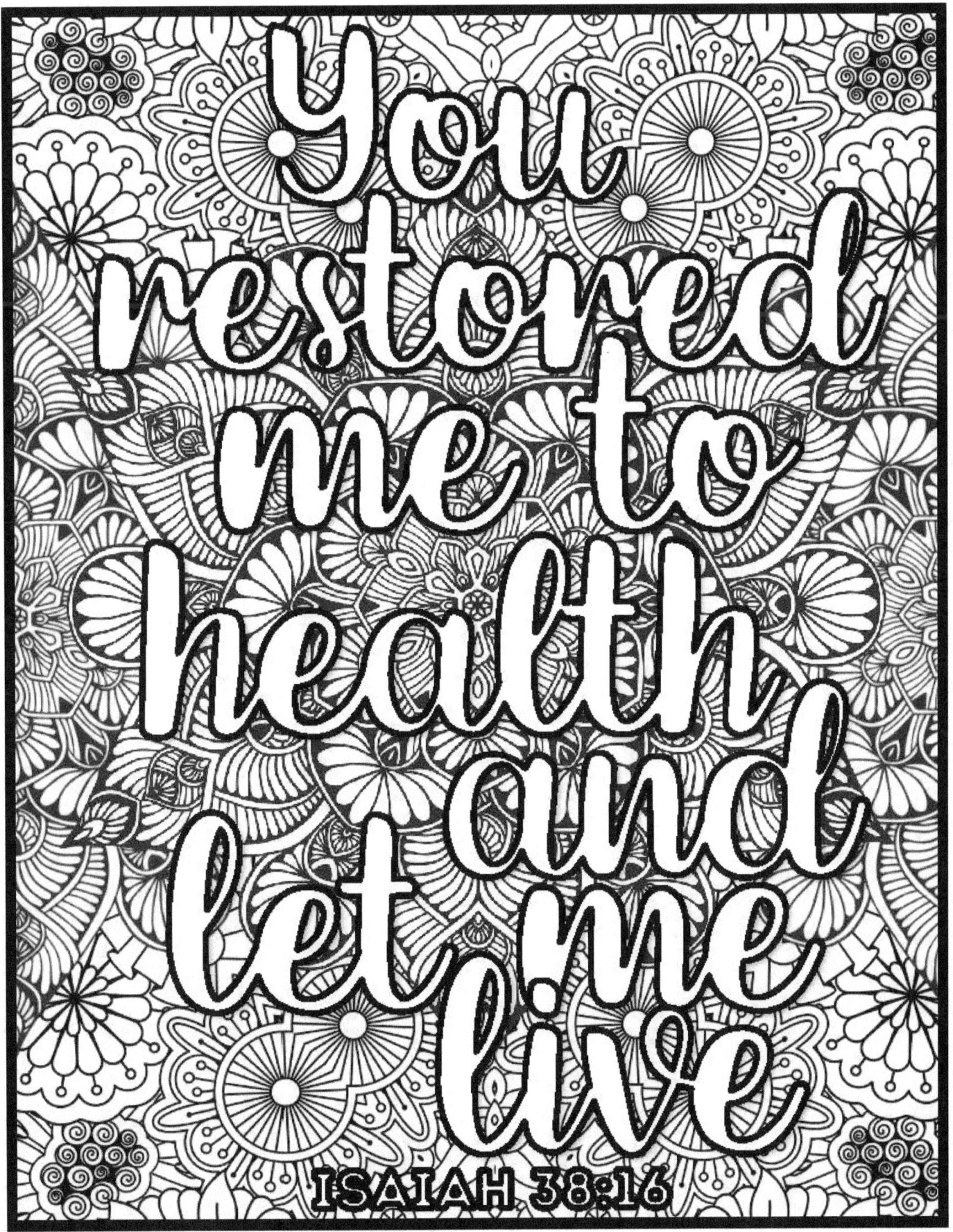

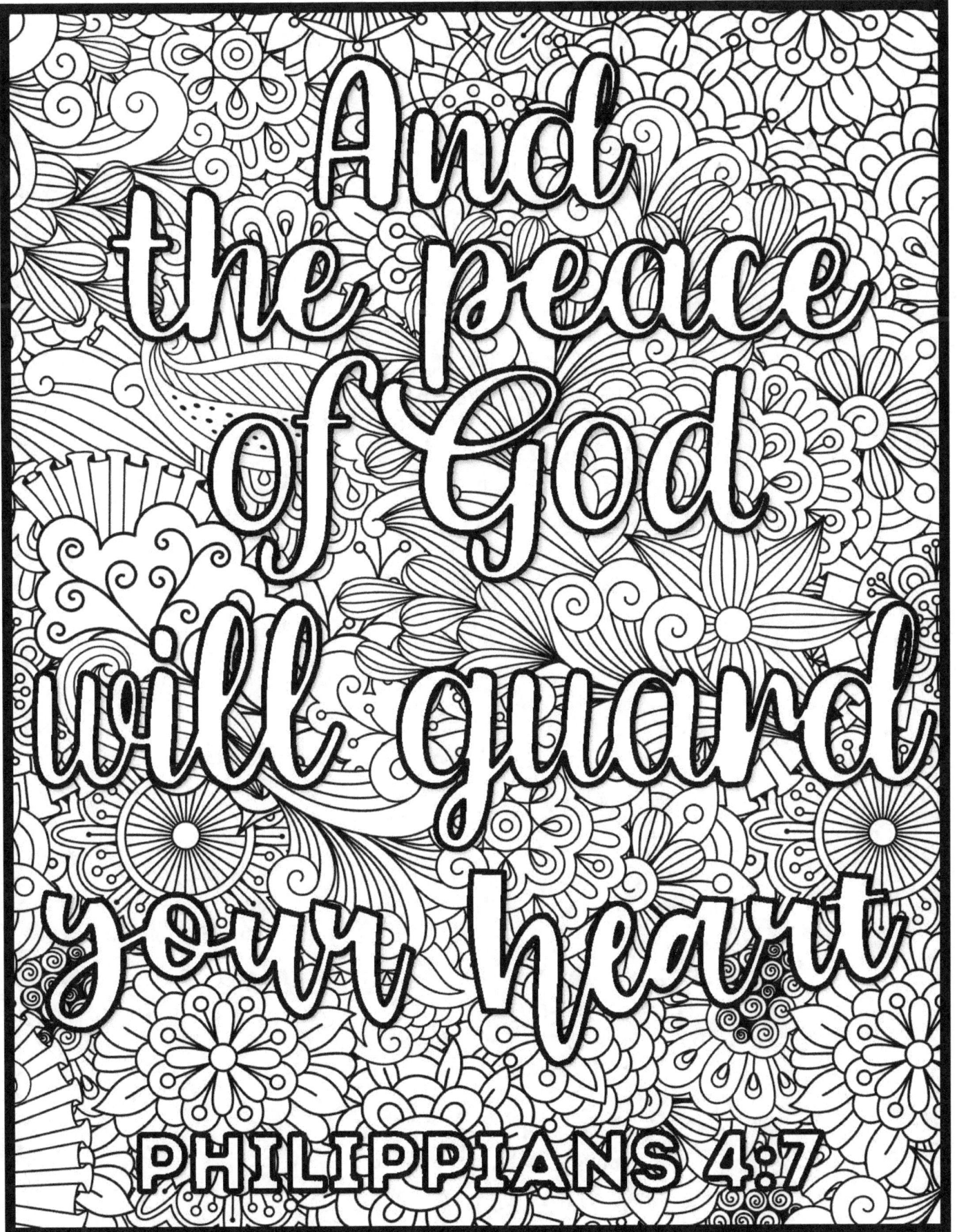

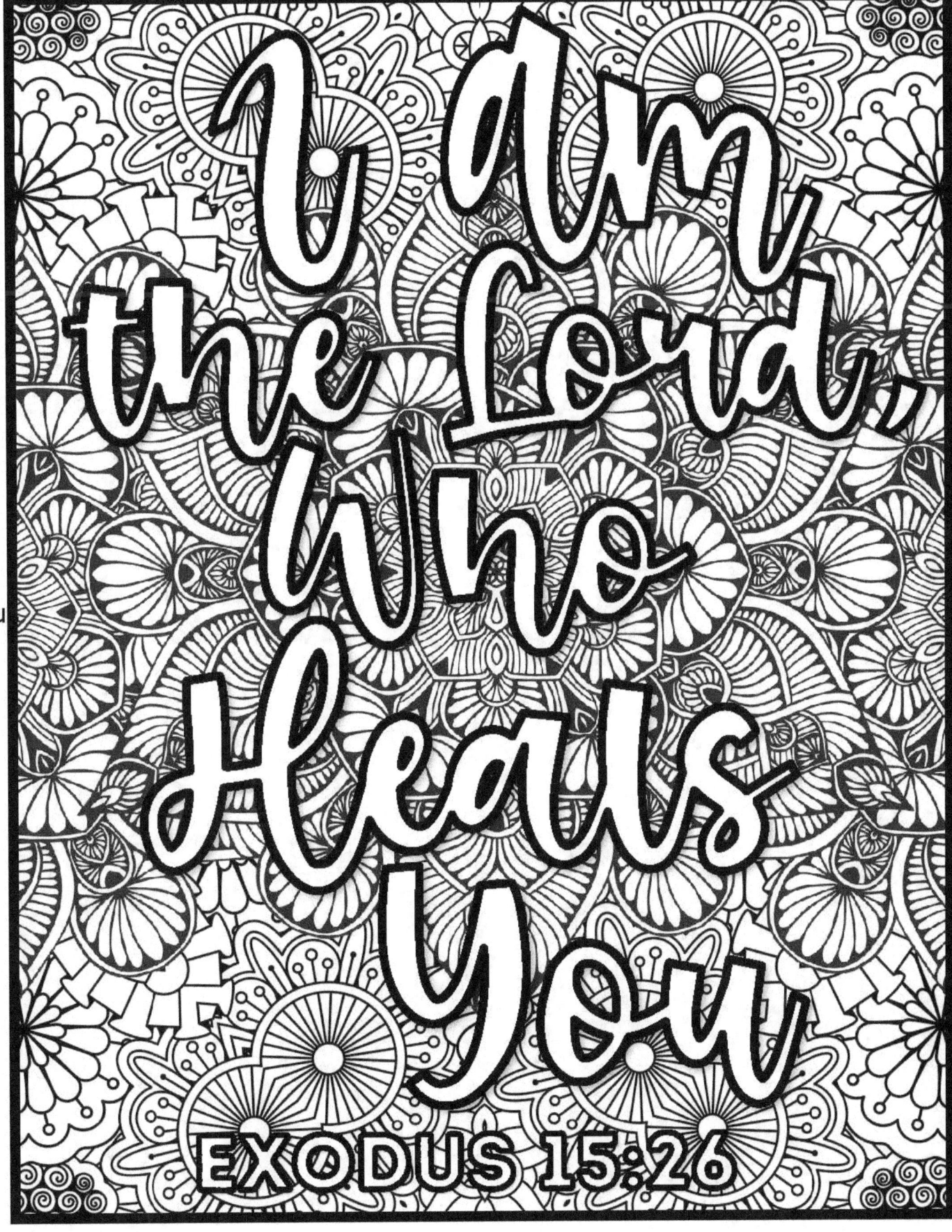

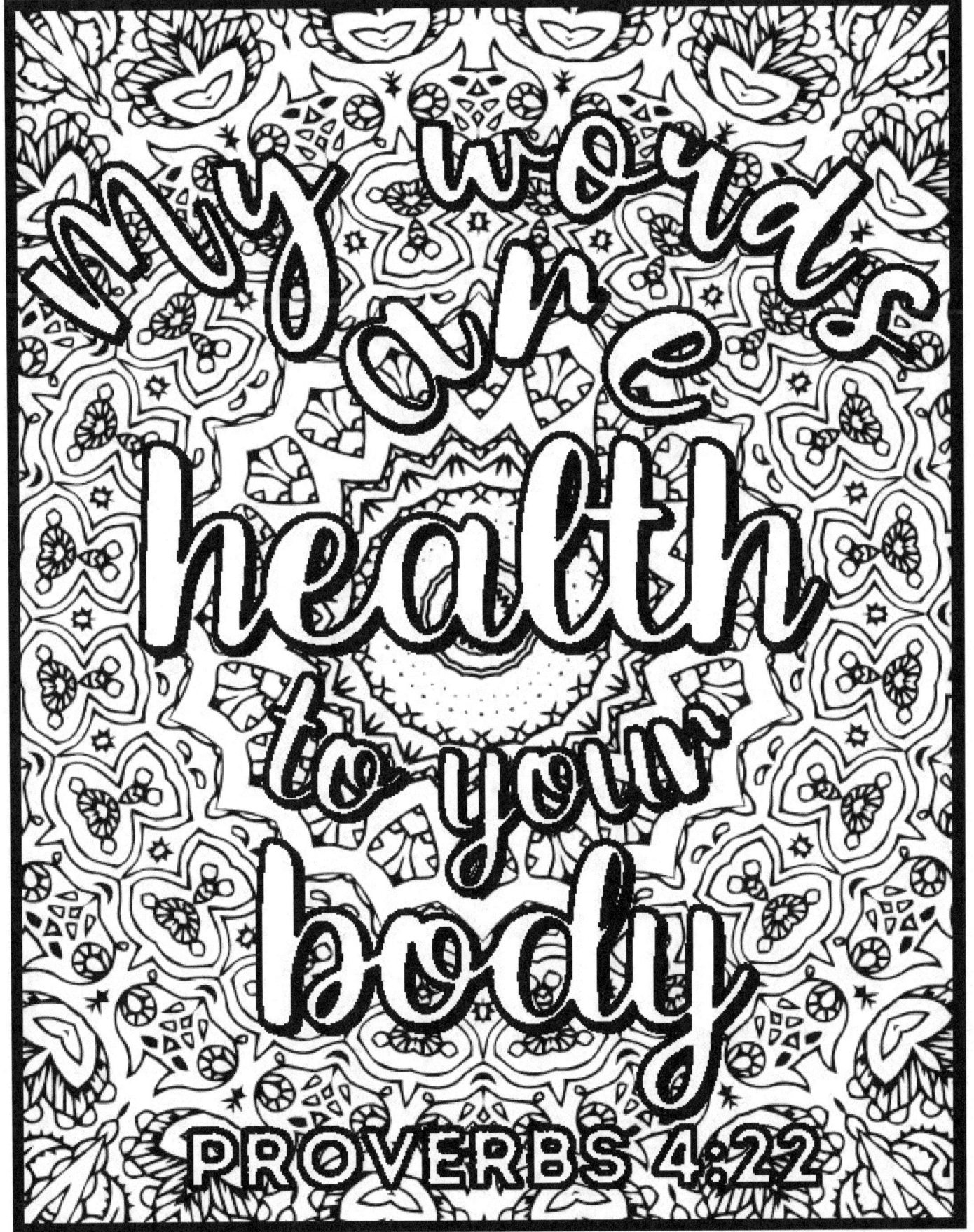

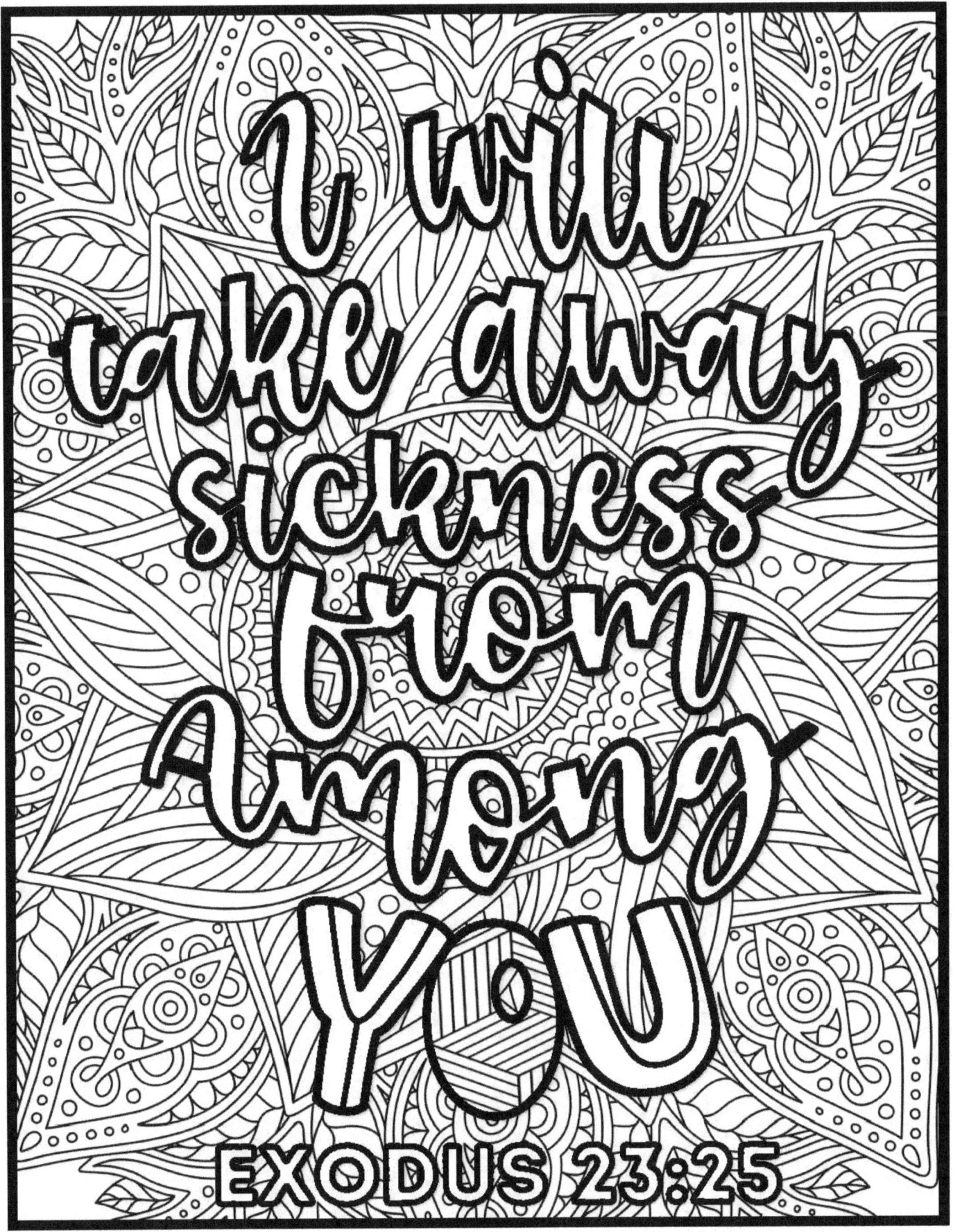

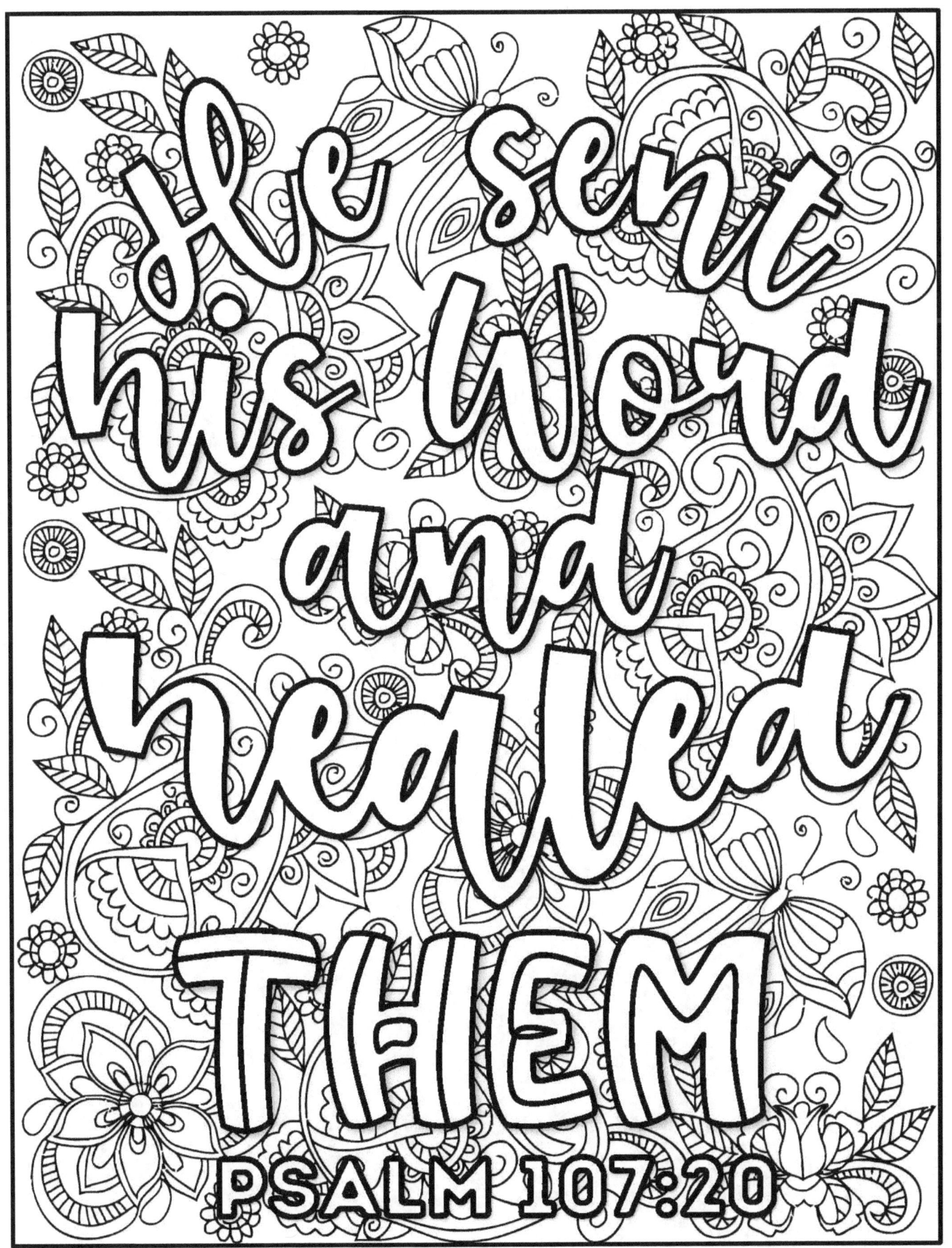

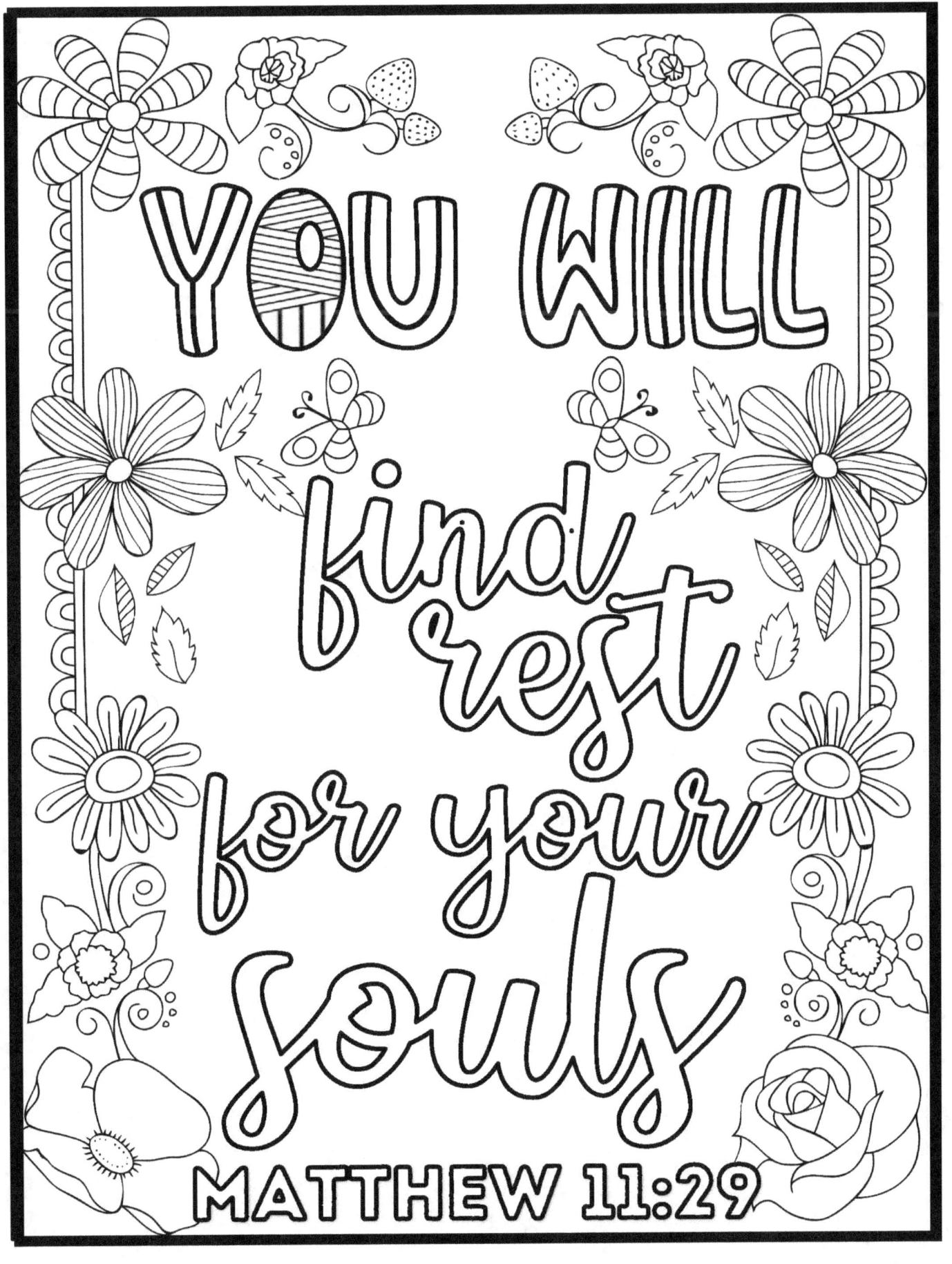

The Lord blesses his people with peace

PSALM 29:11

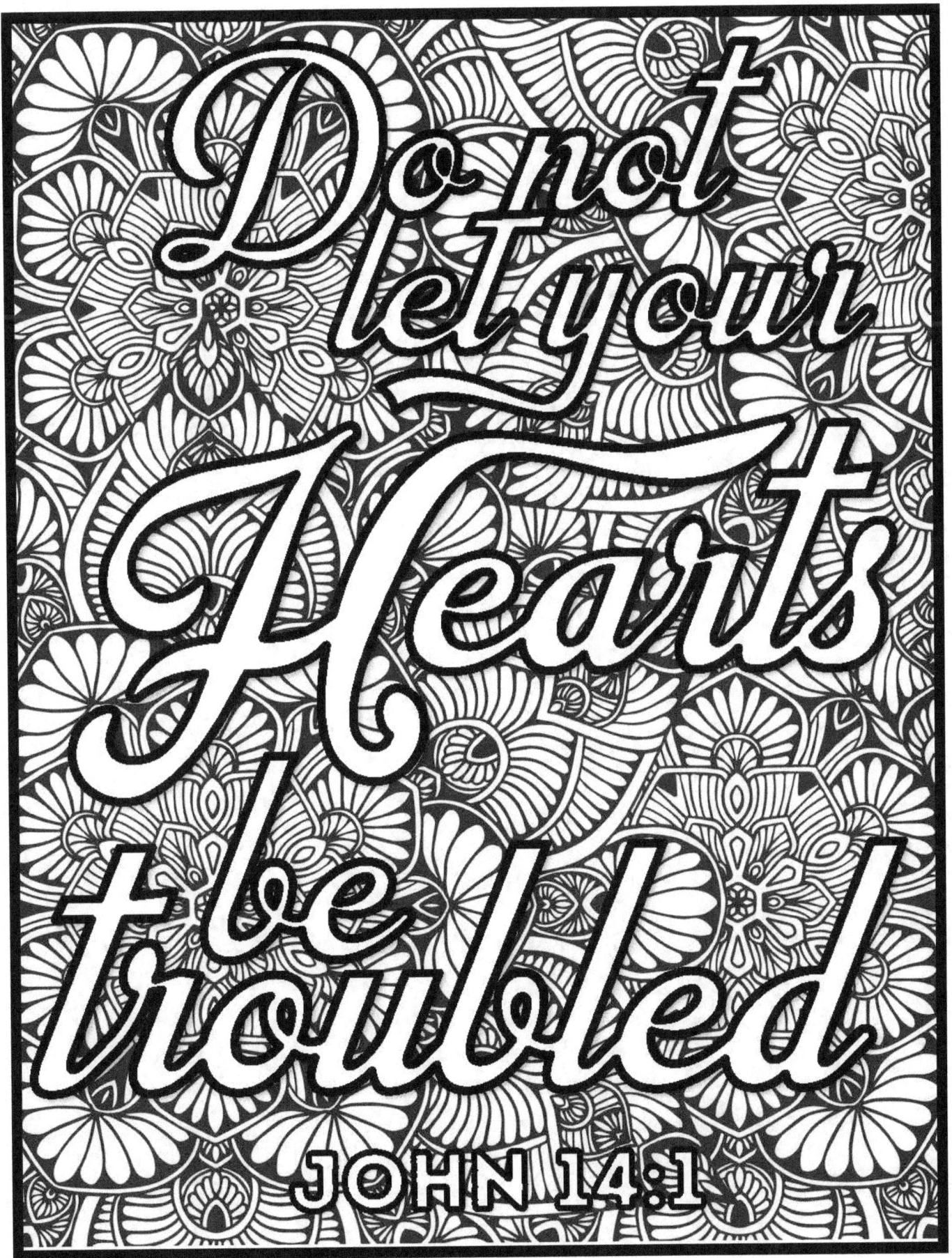

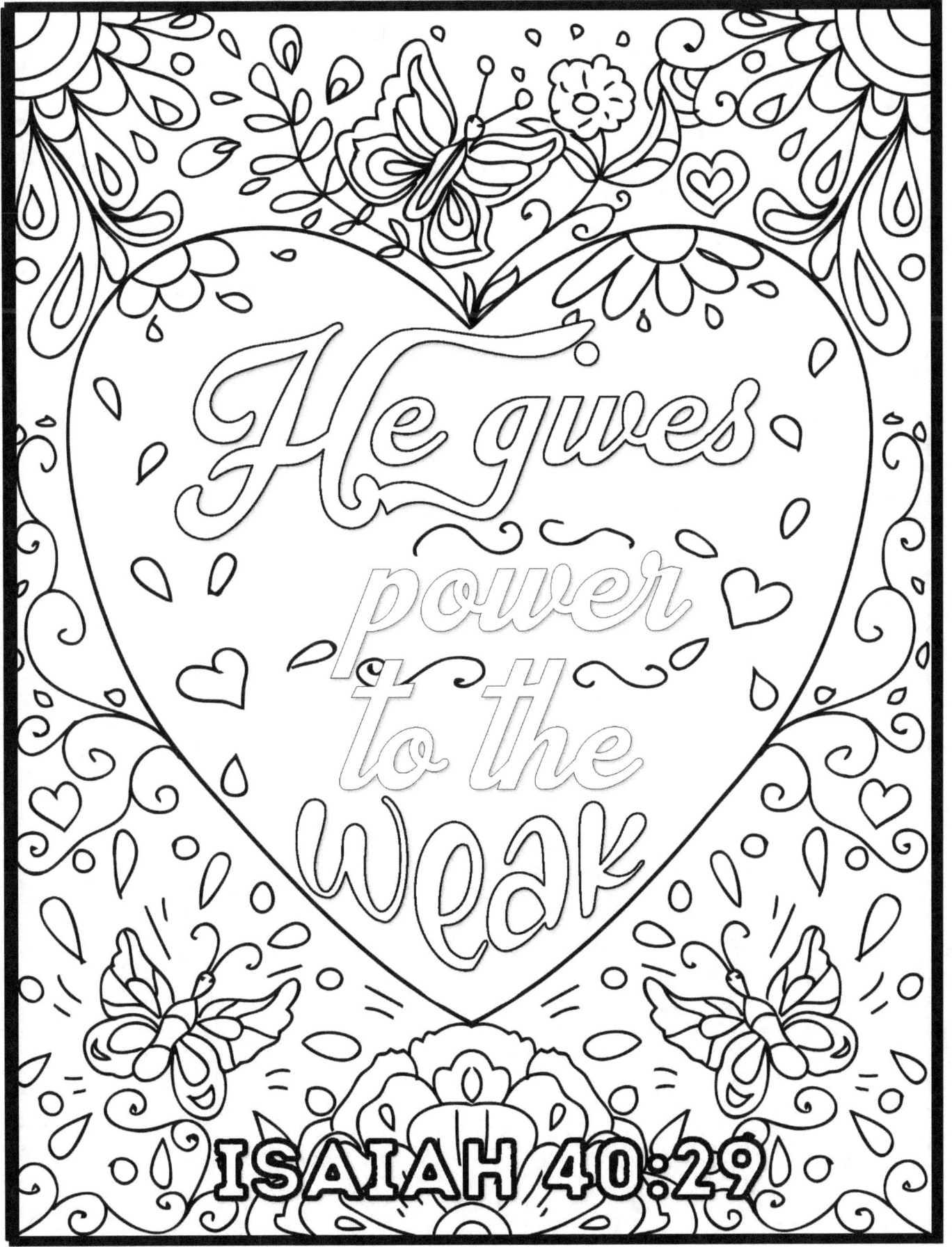

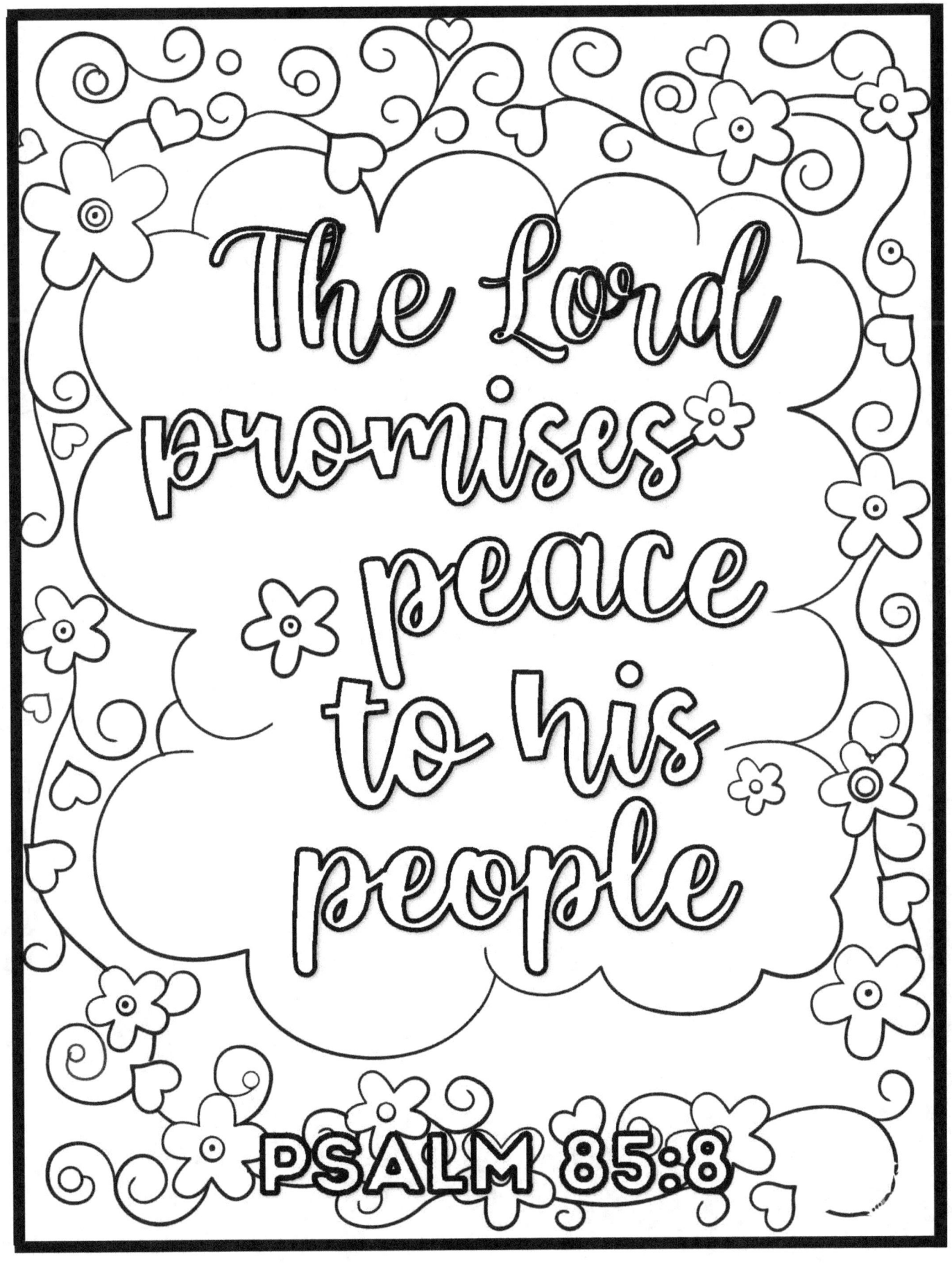

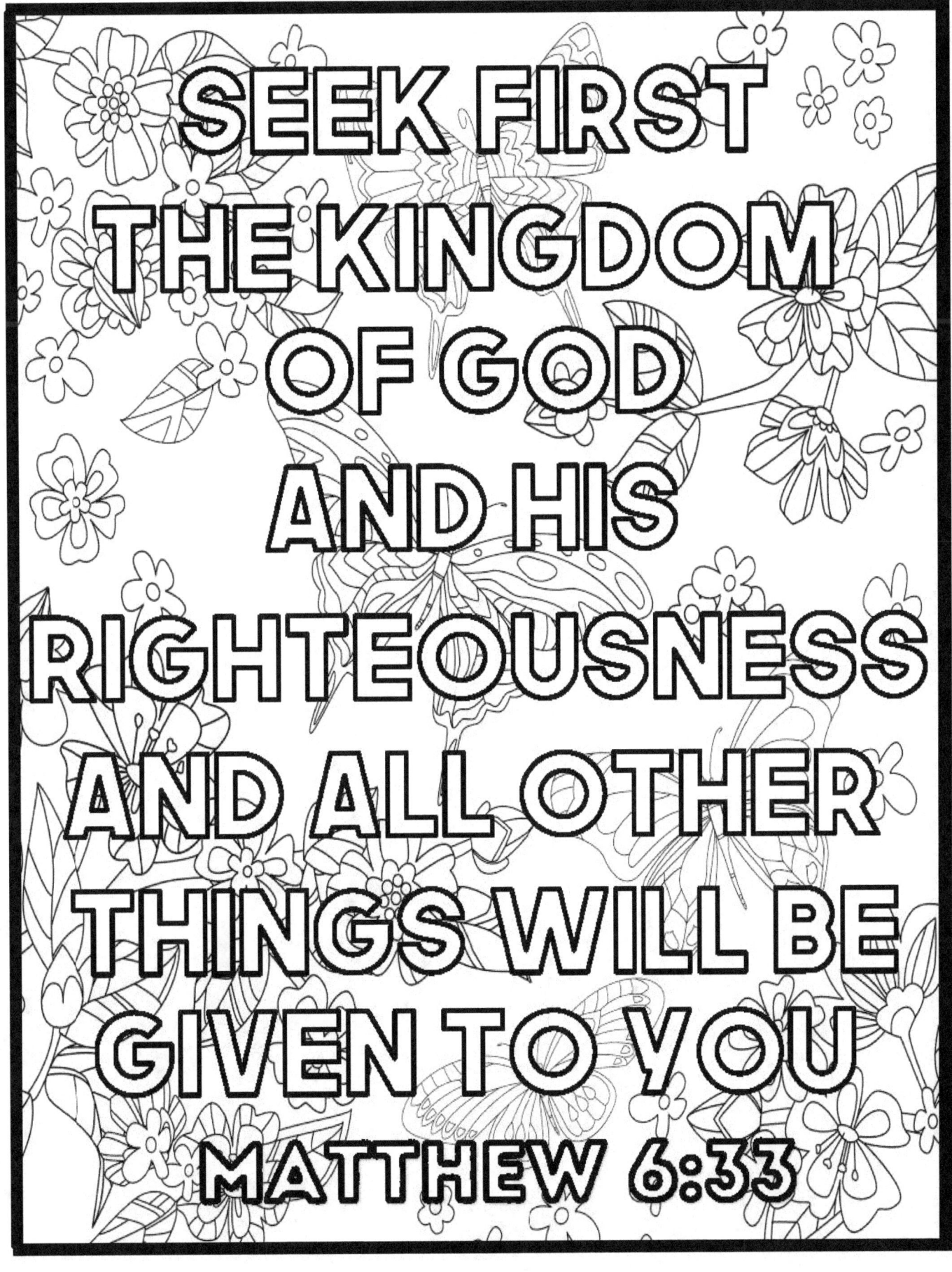

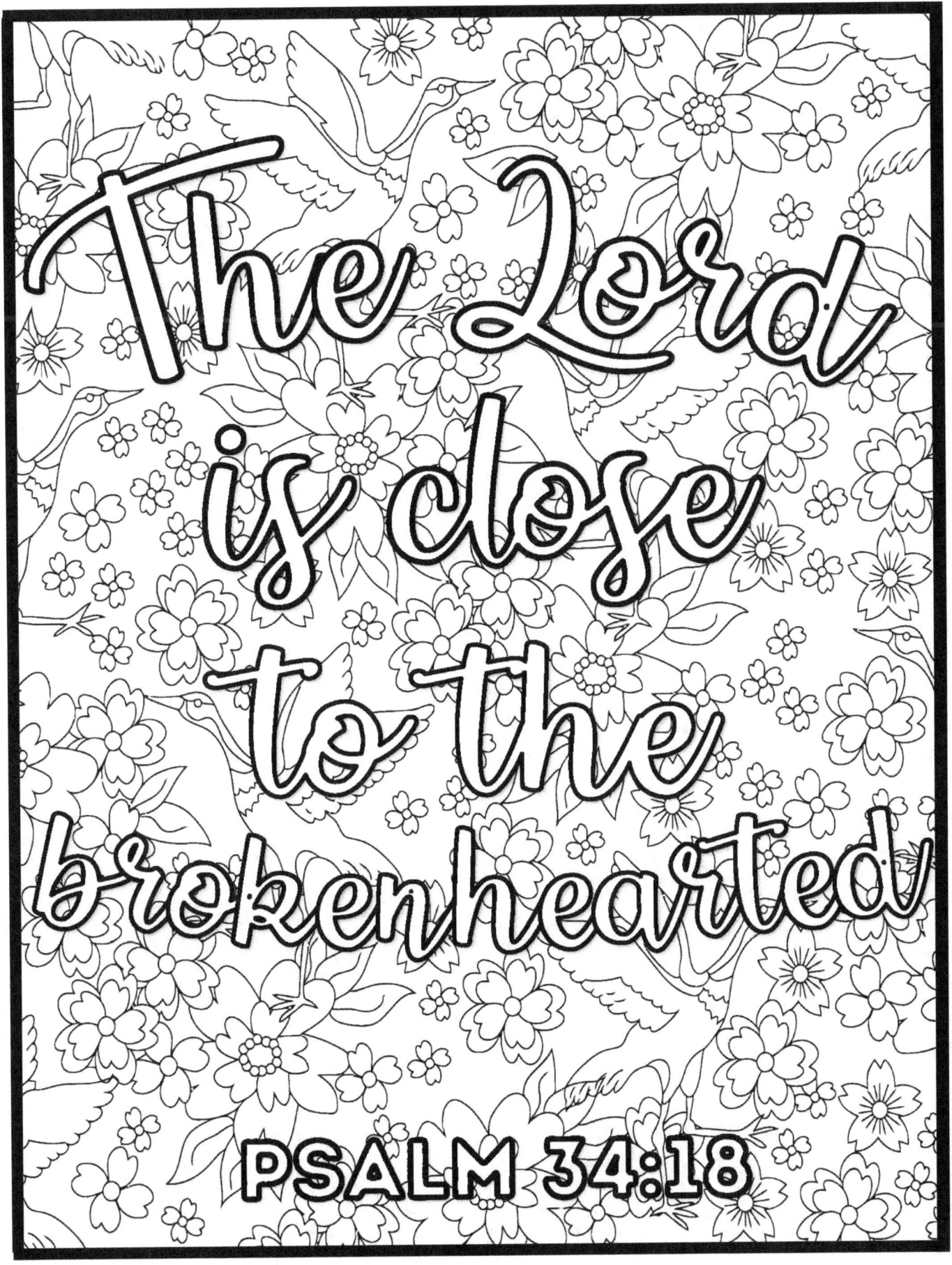

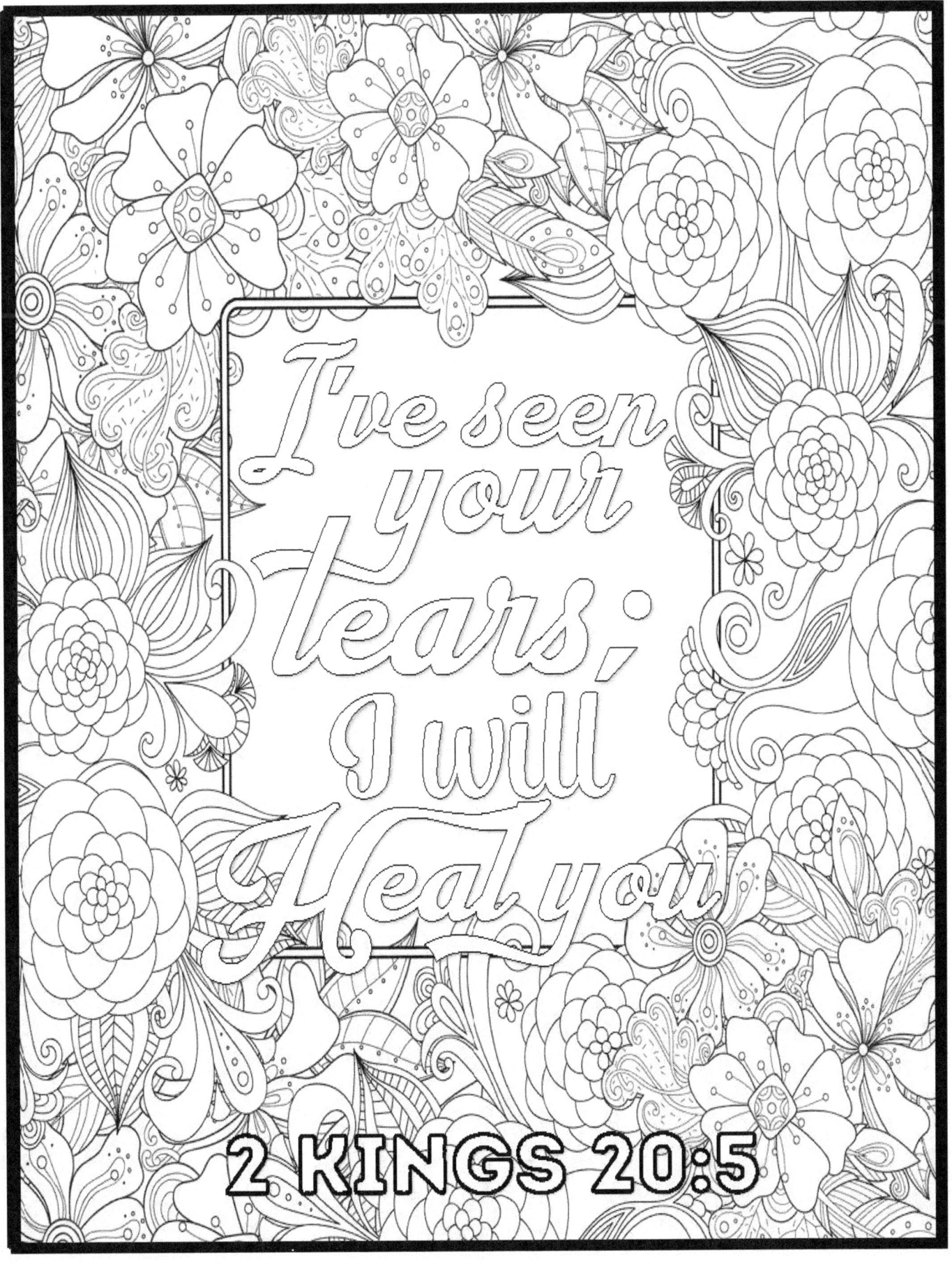

Heal me, Lord, and I will be HEALED
JEREMIAH 17:14

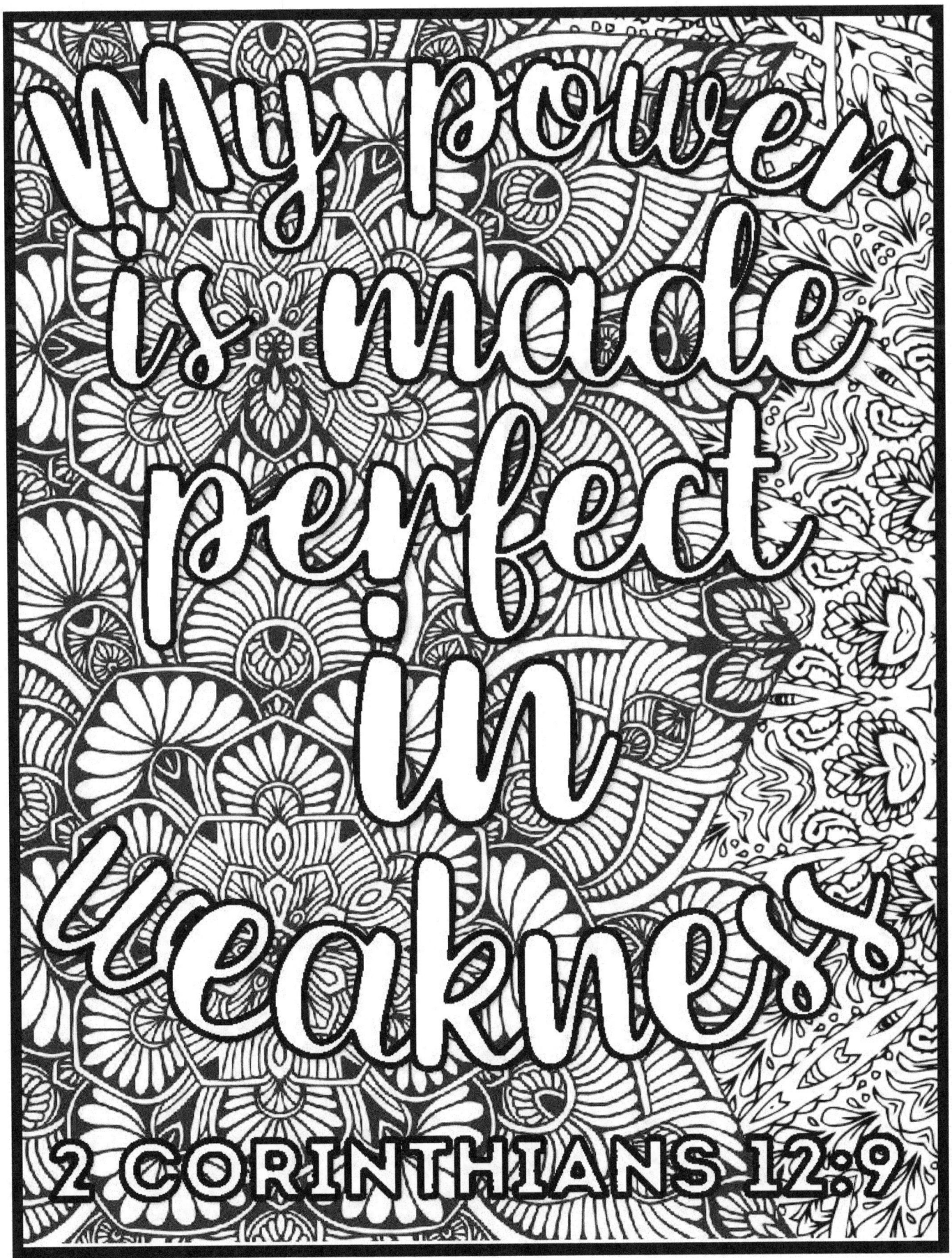

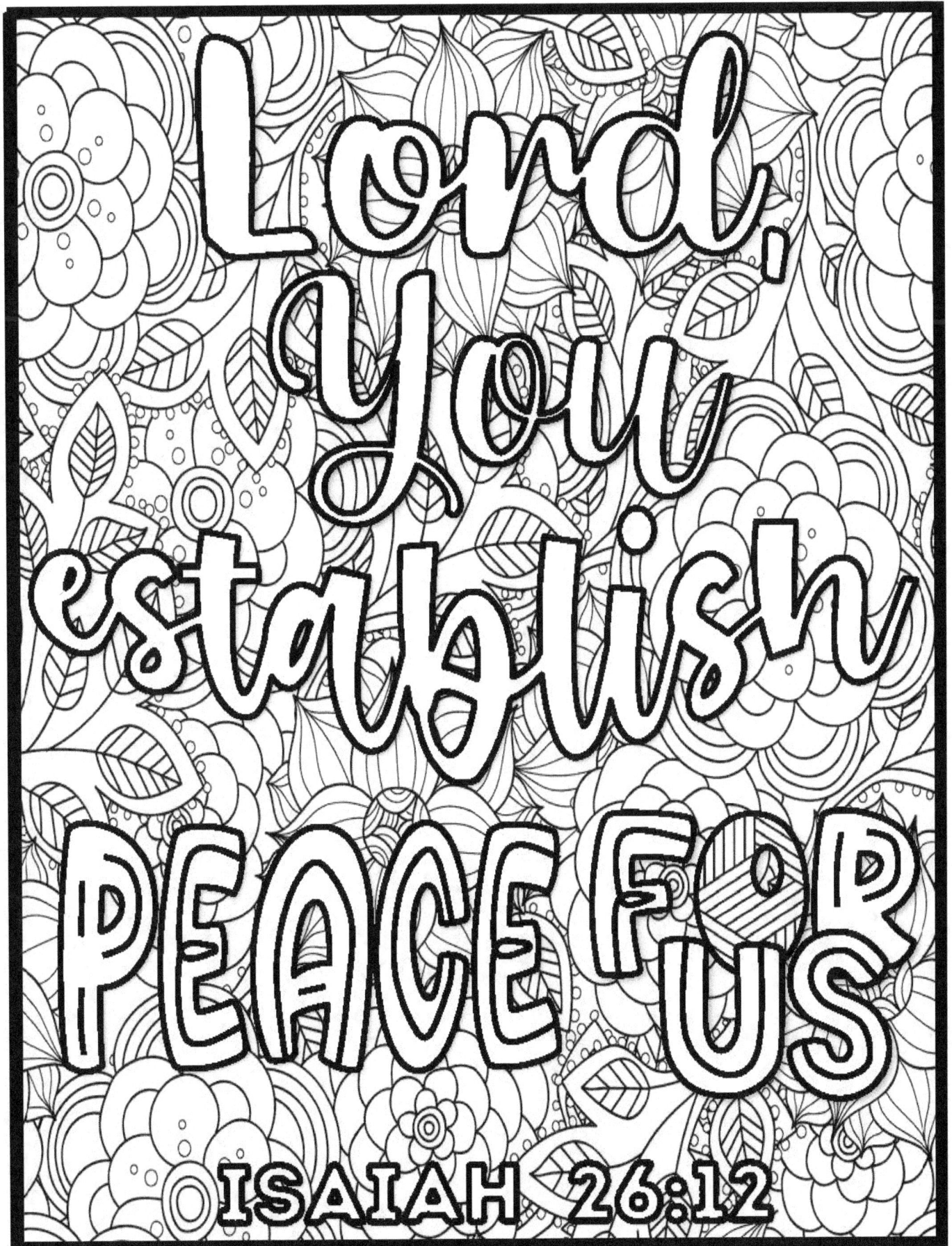

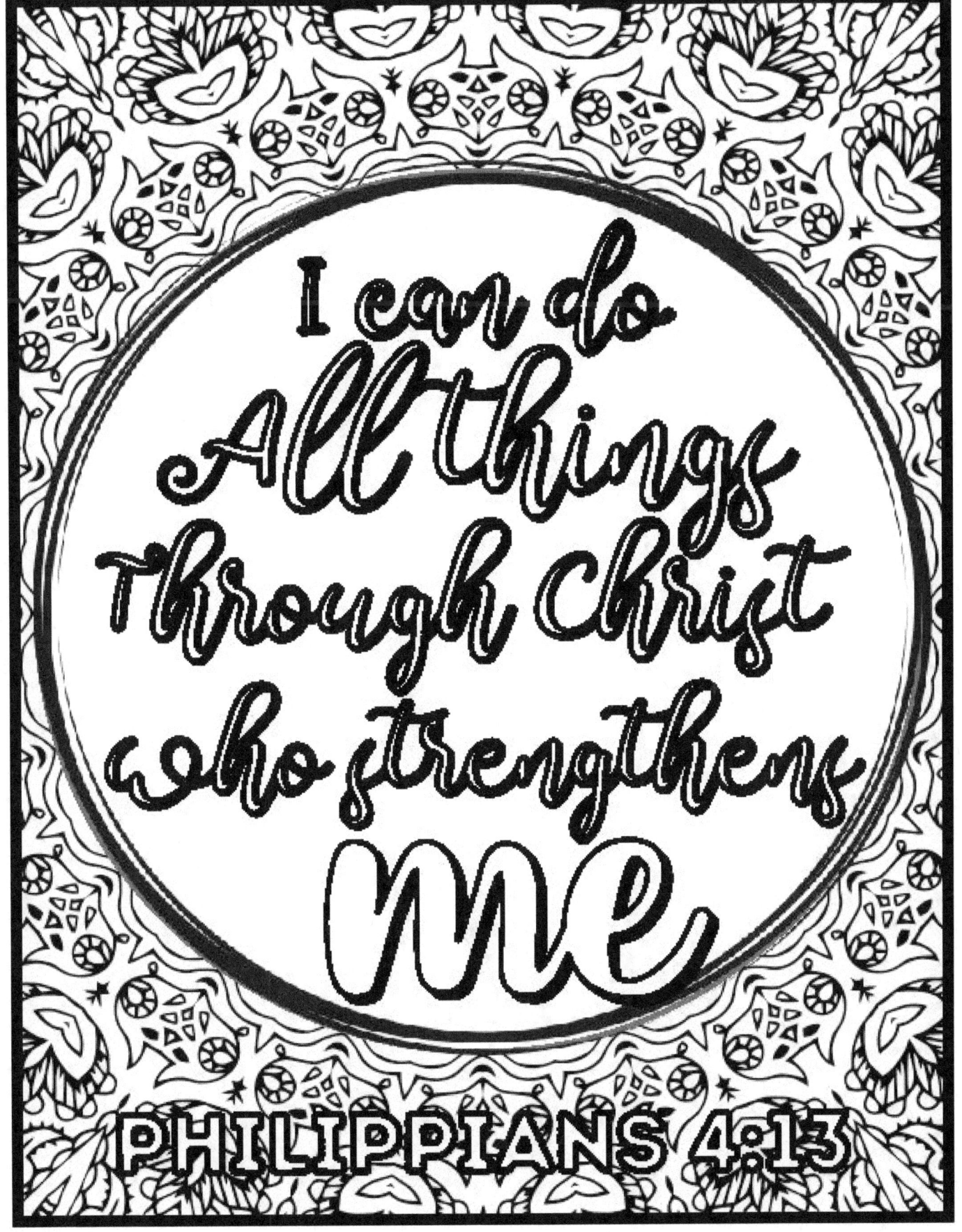

You shall love the Lord your God with all your heart, with all your soul, and with all your strength

DEUTERONOMY 6:5

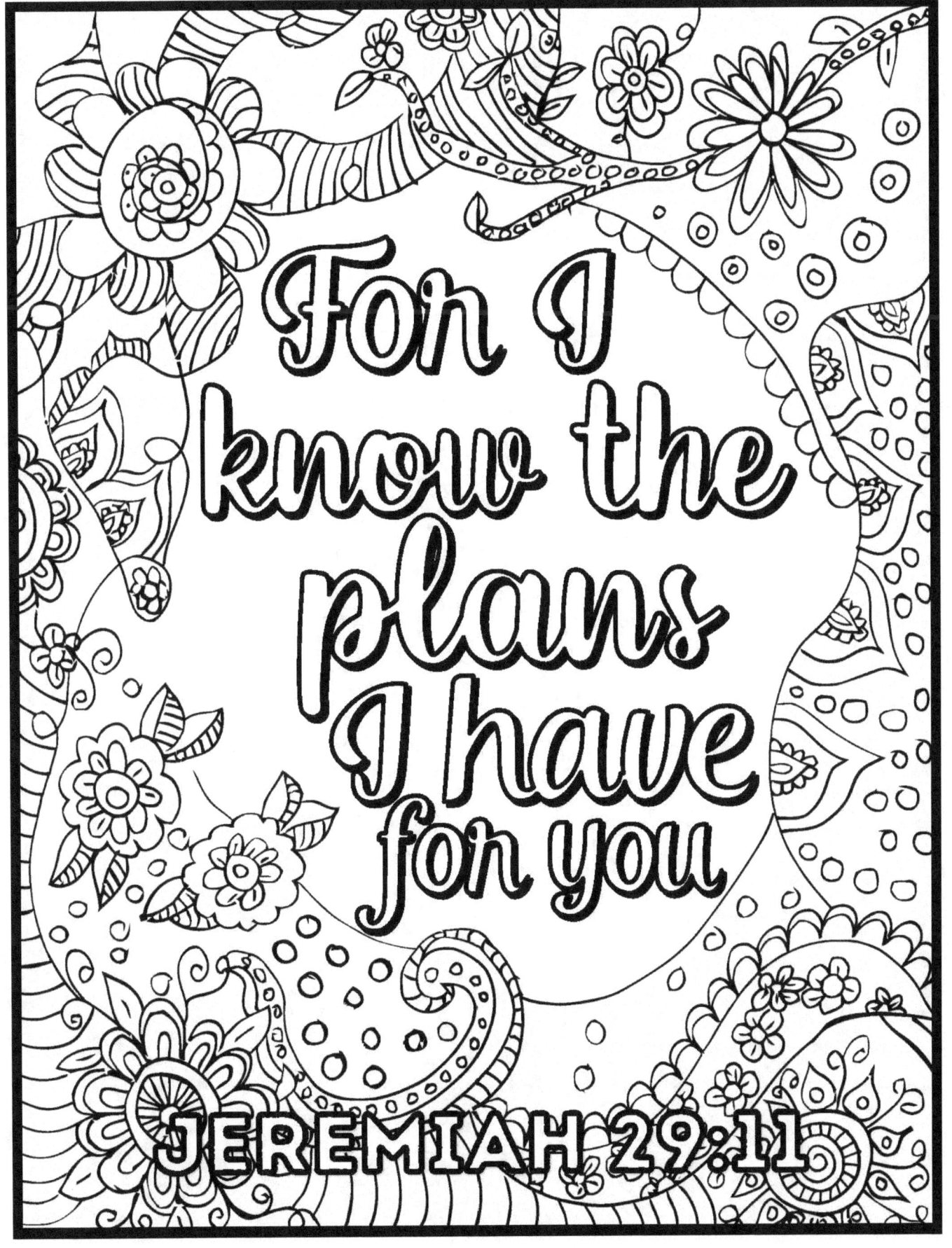

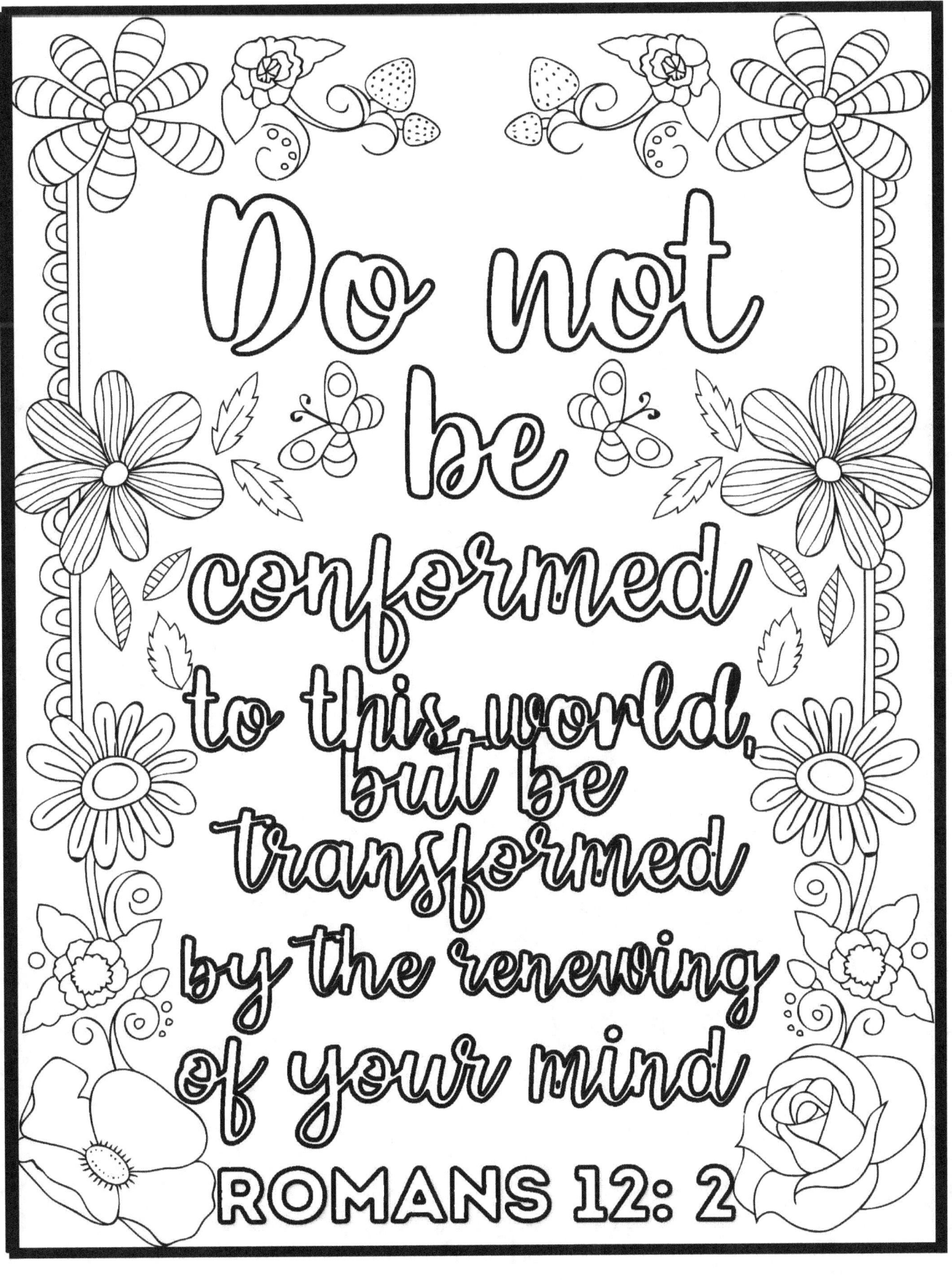

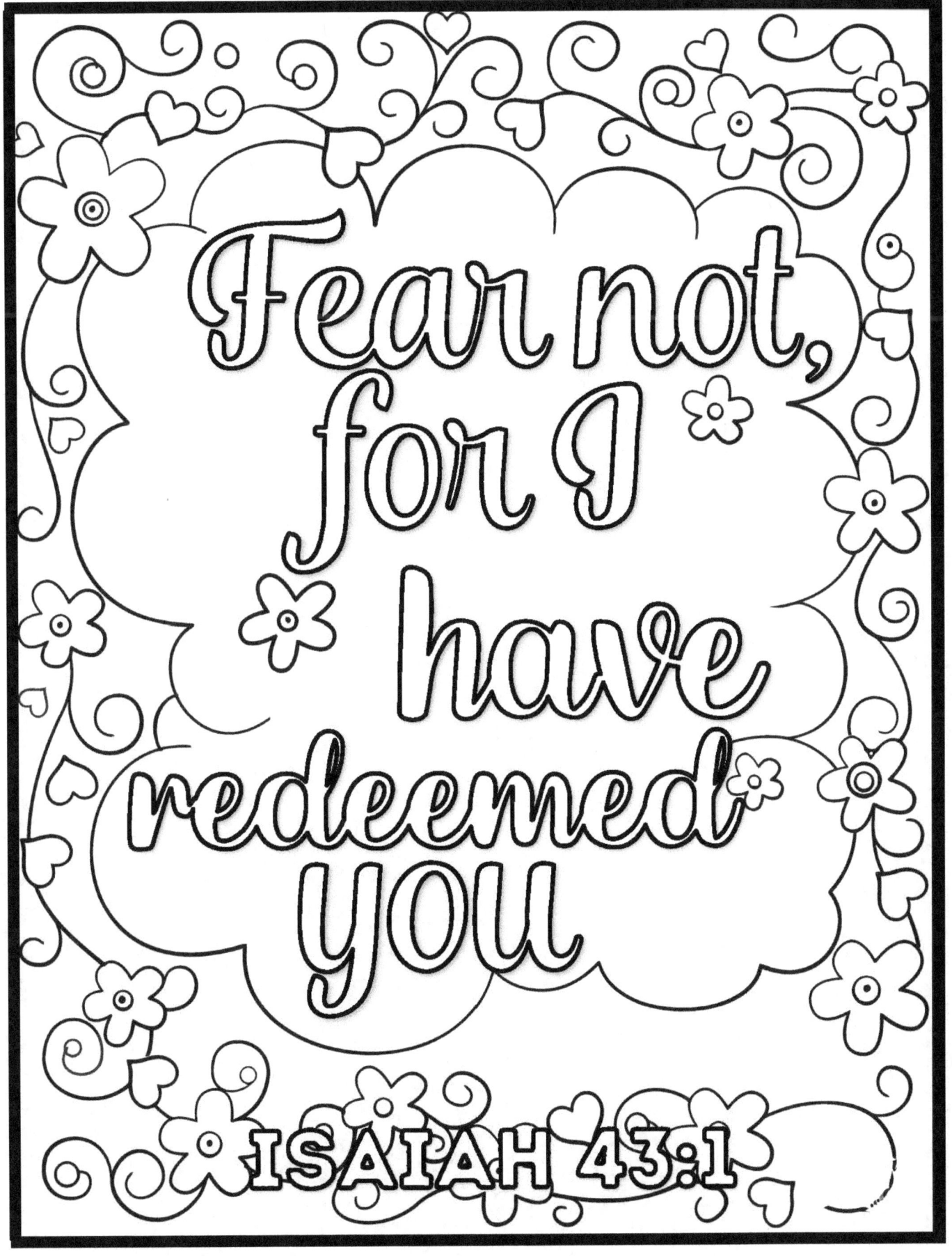

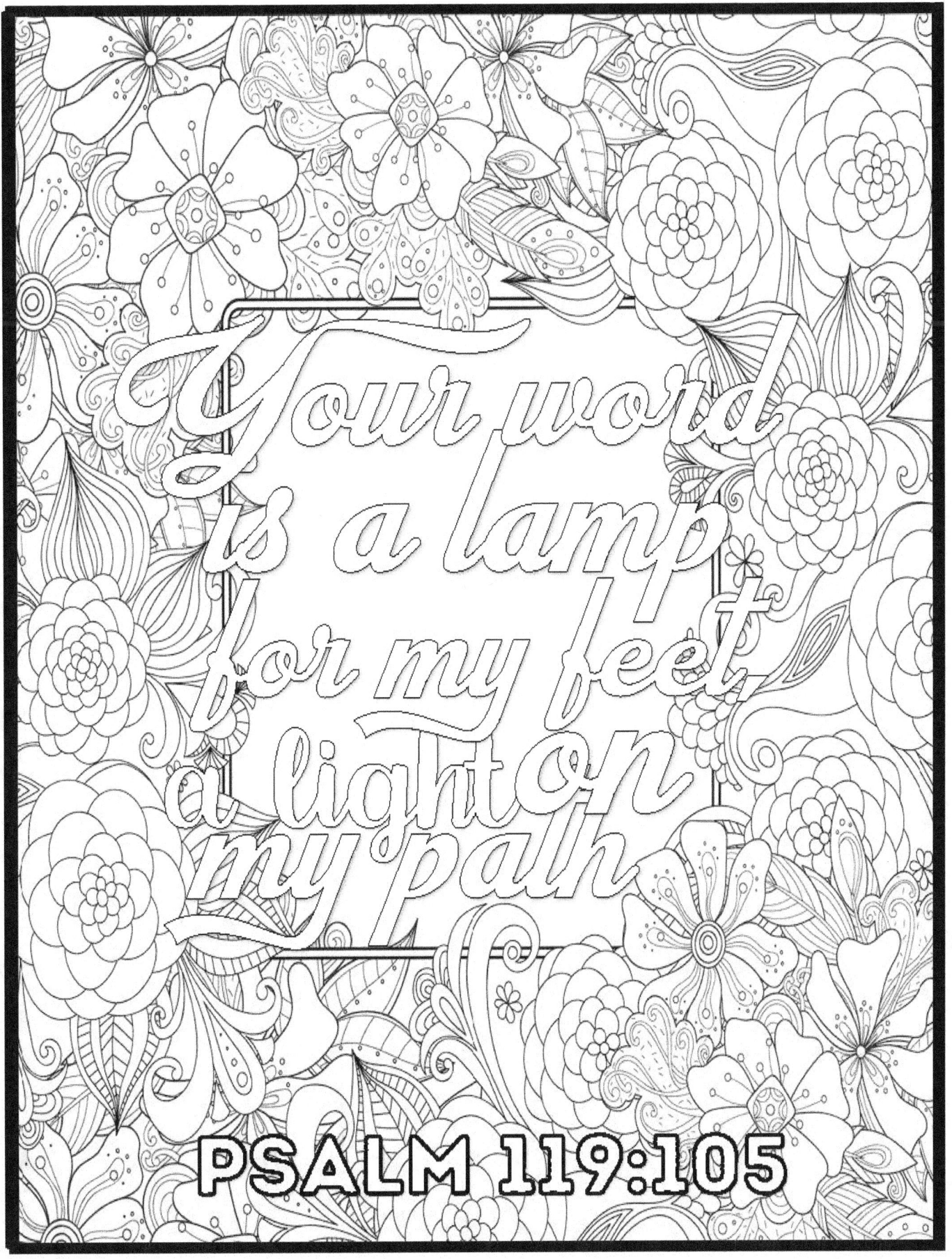

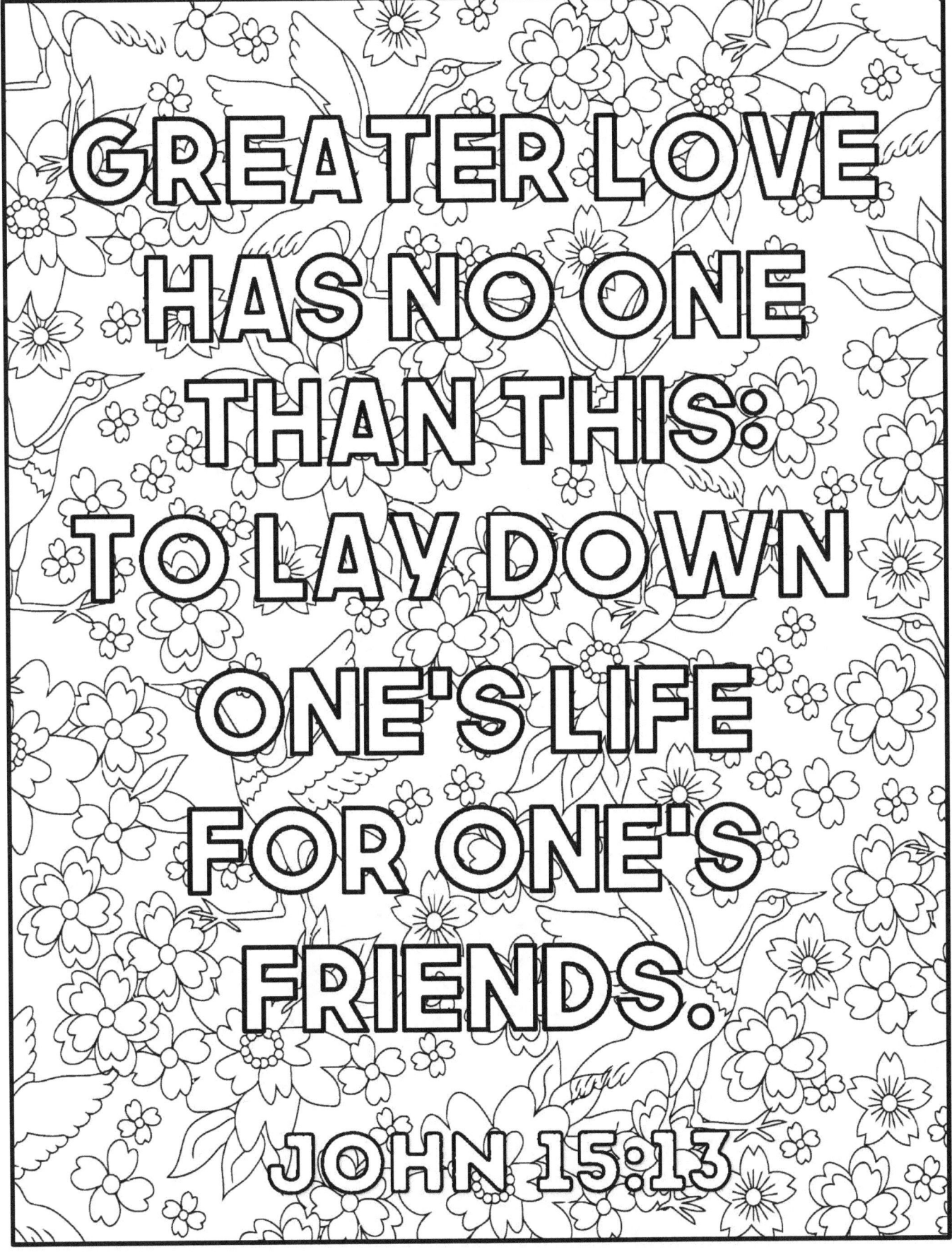

What, then, shall we say in response to these things? If God is for us, who can be against us?

ROMANS 8:31

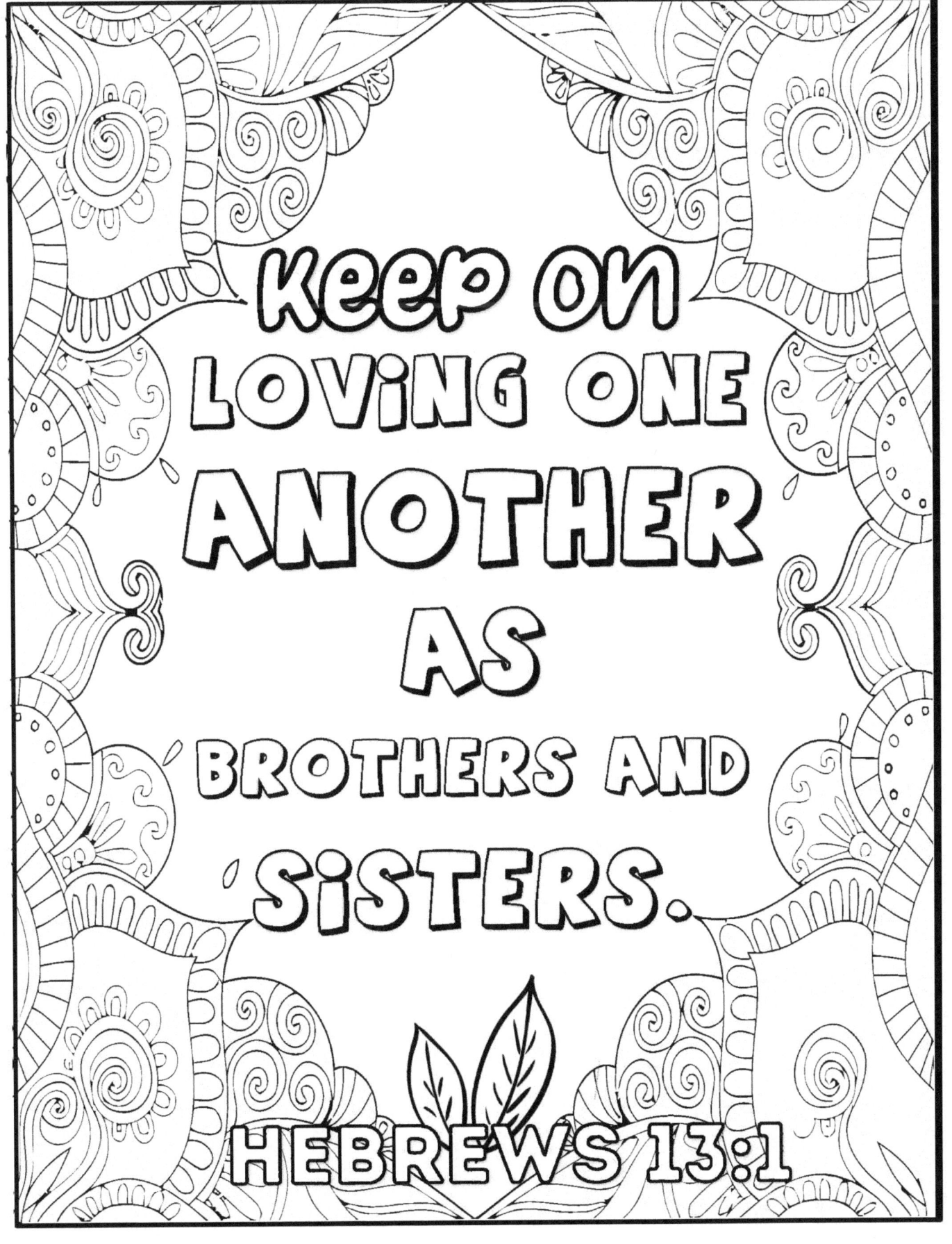

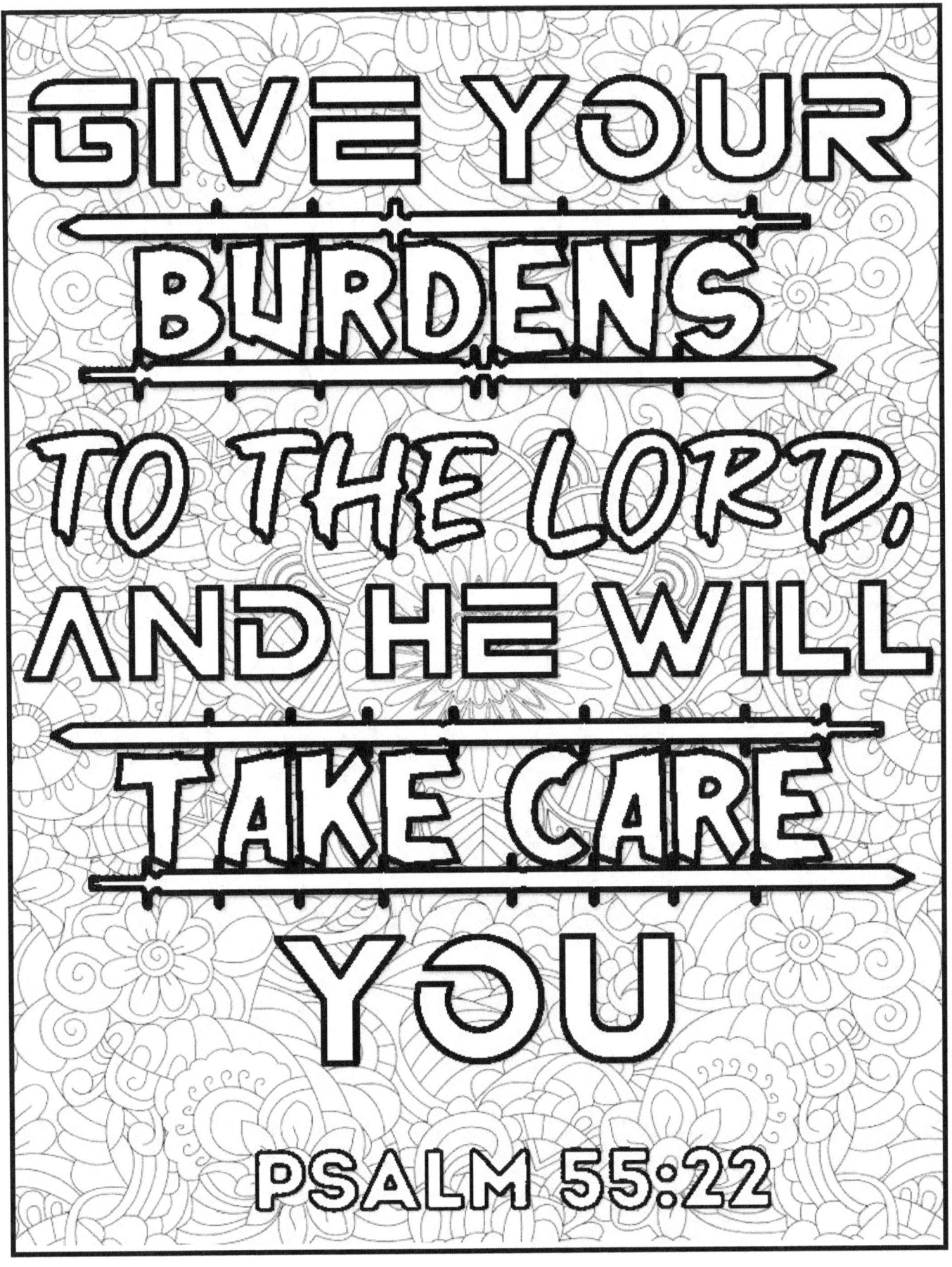

For with God nothing will be impossible

Luke 1:37

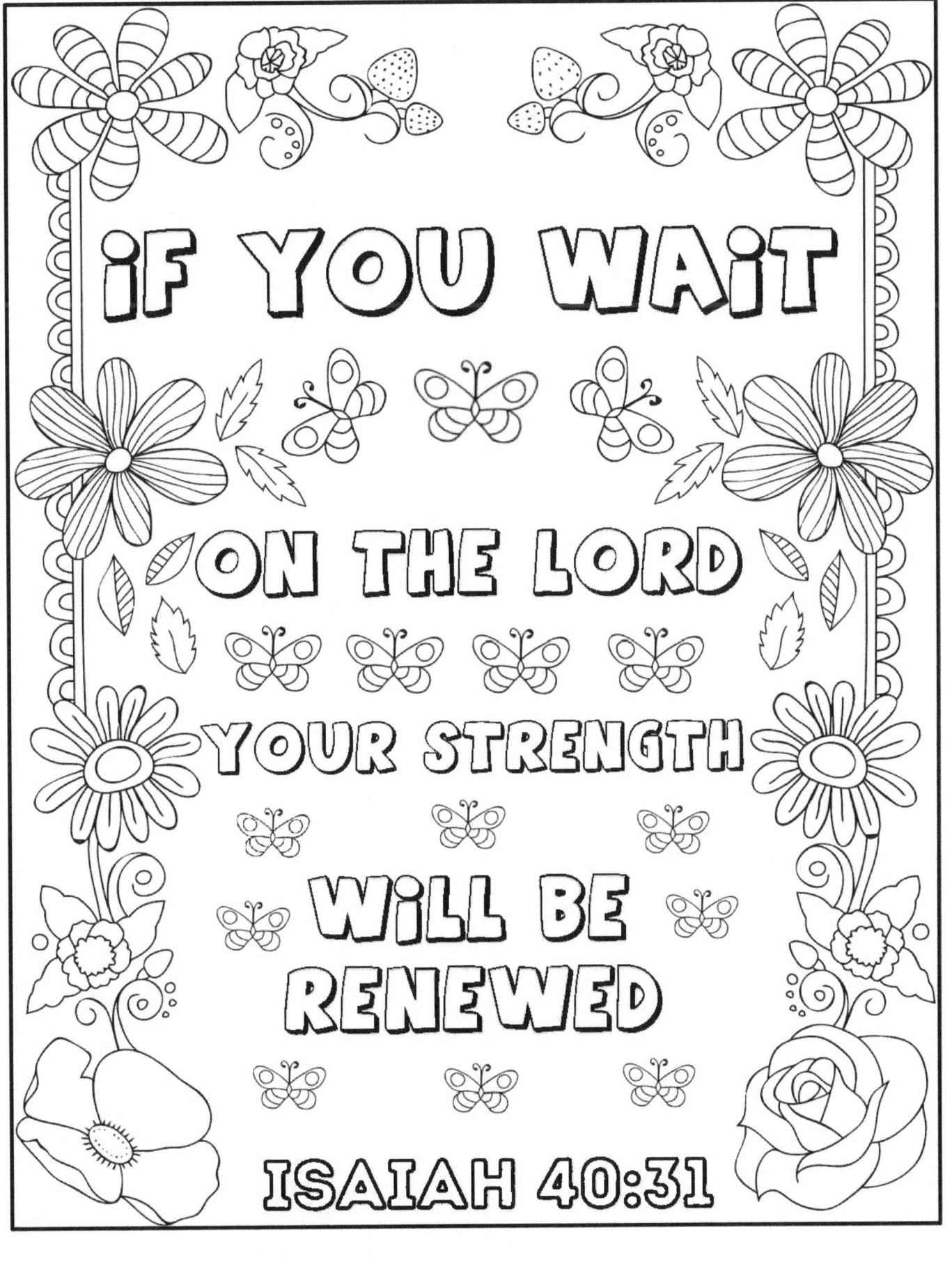

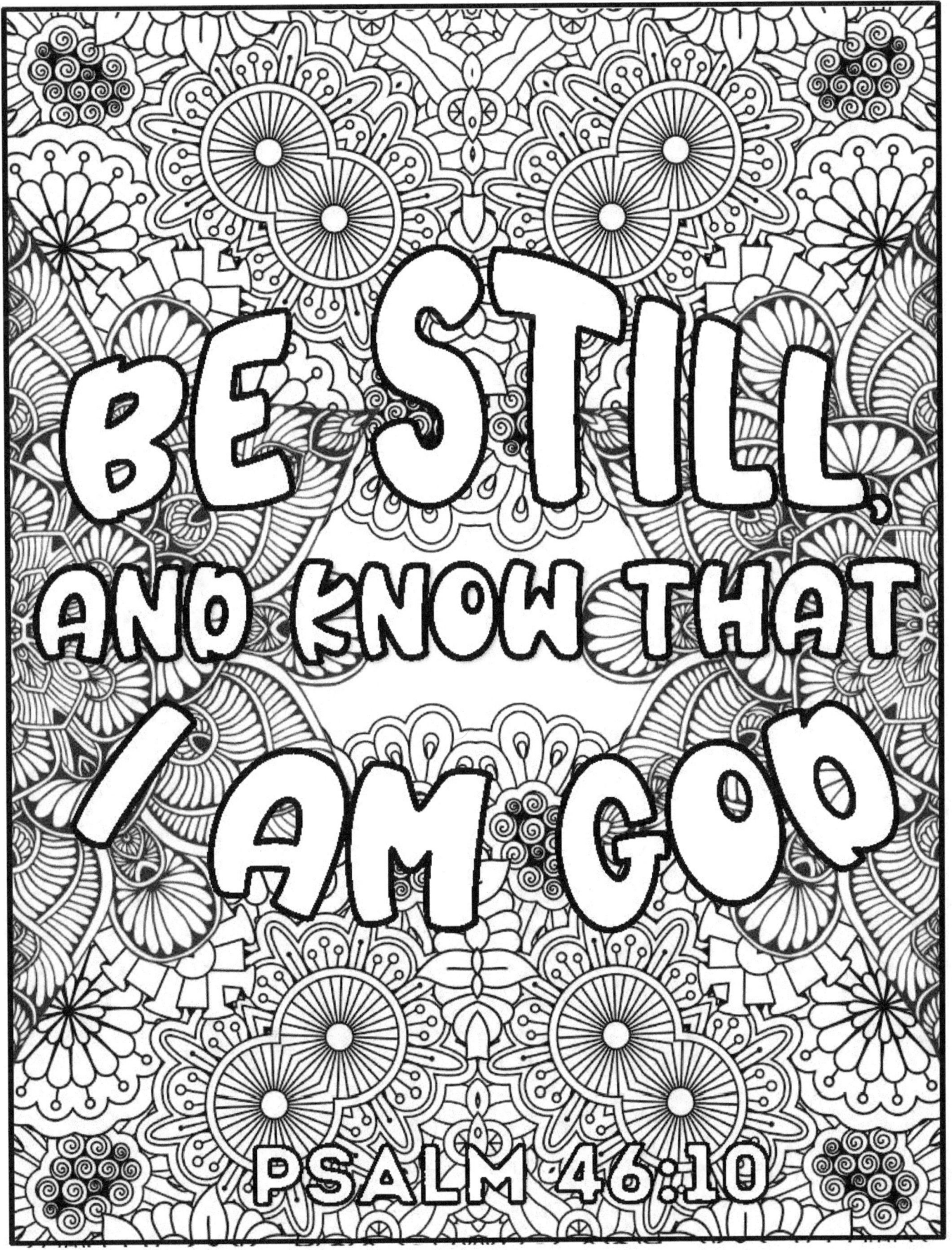

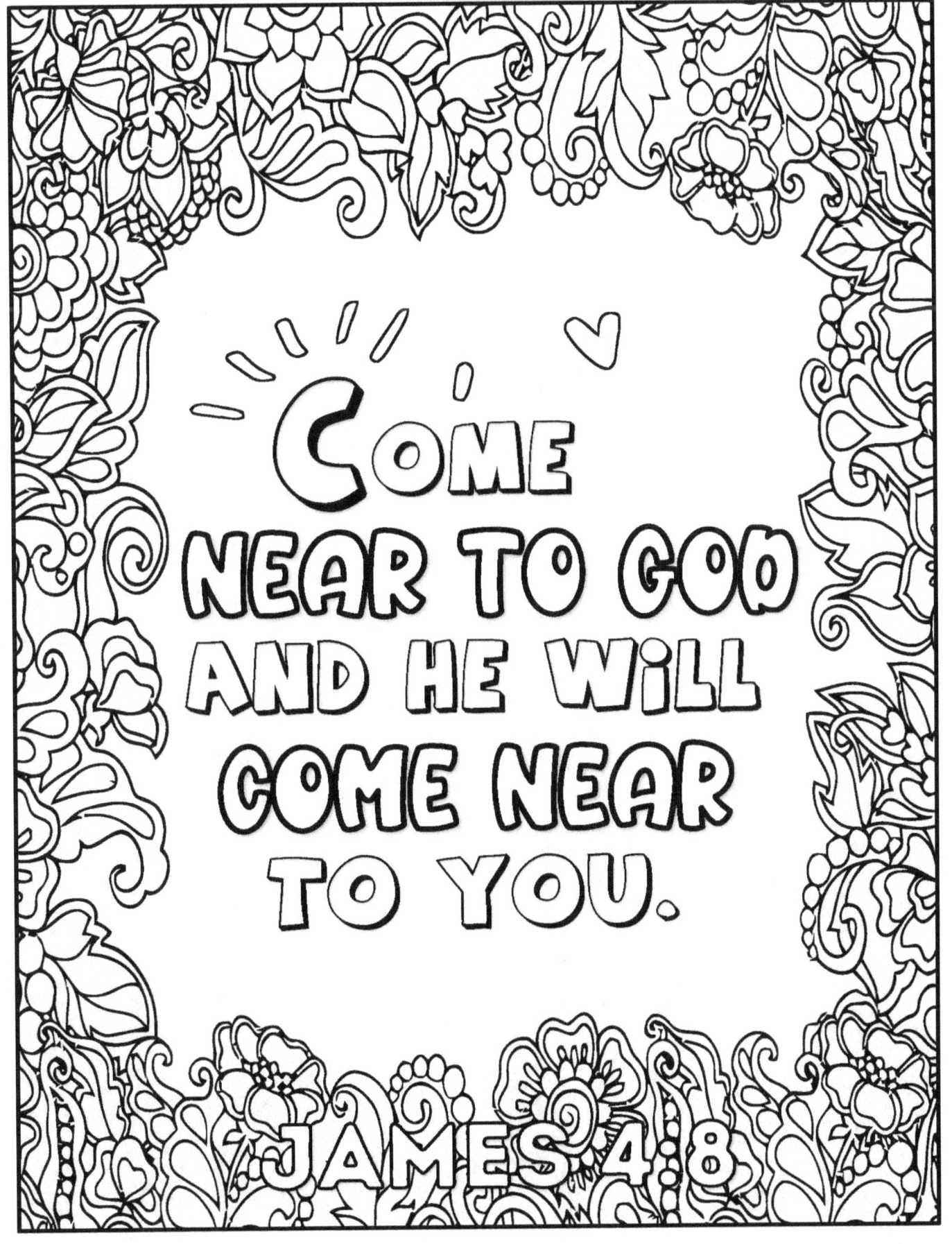

I am with you will watch over you wherever you go

GENESIS 28:15

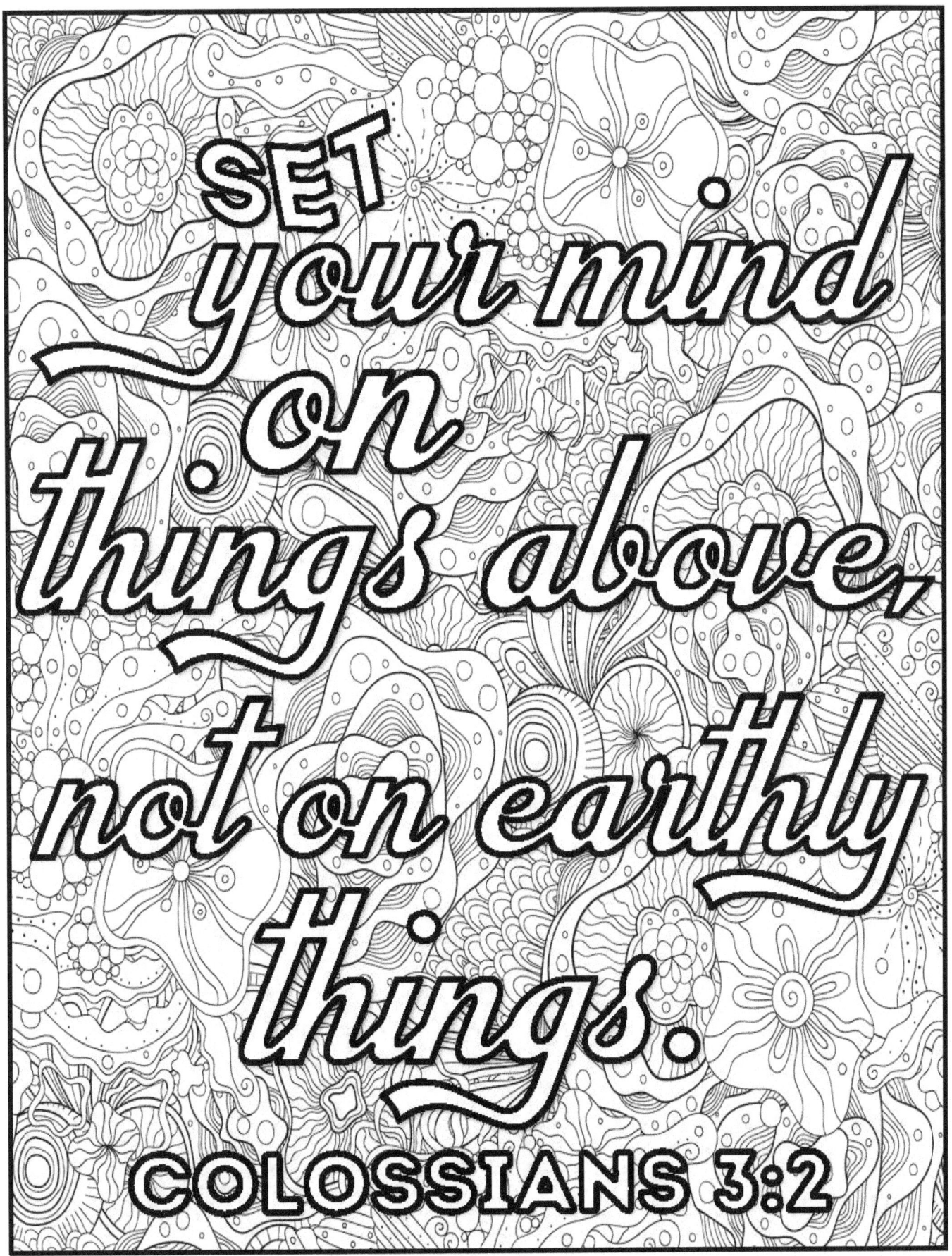

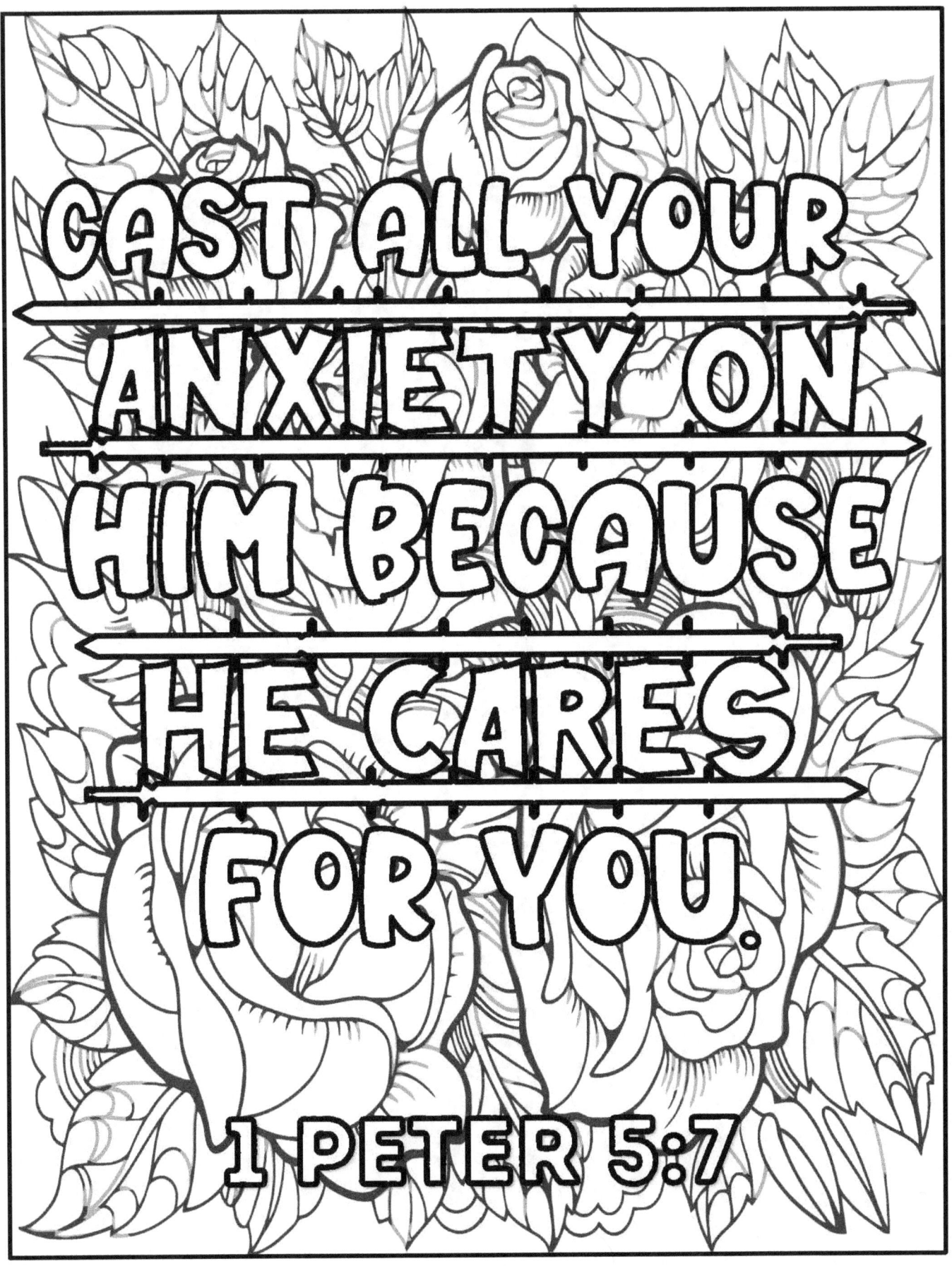

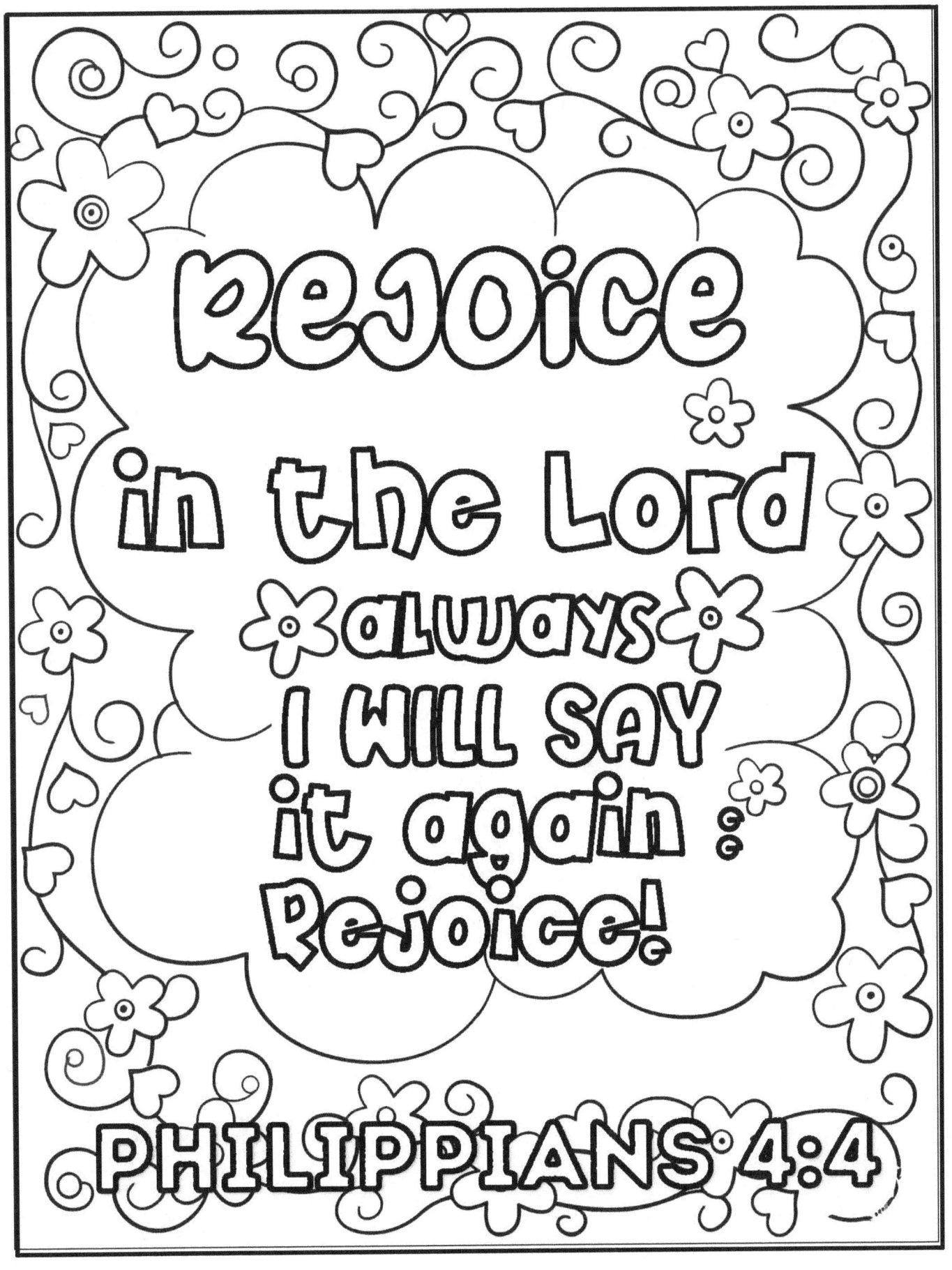

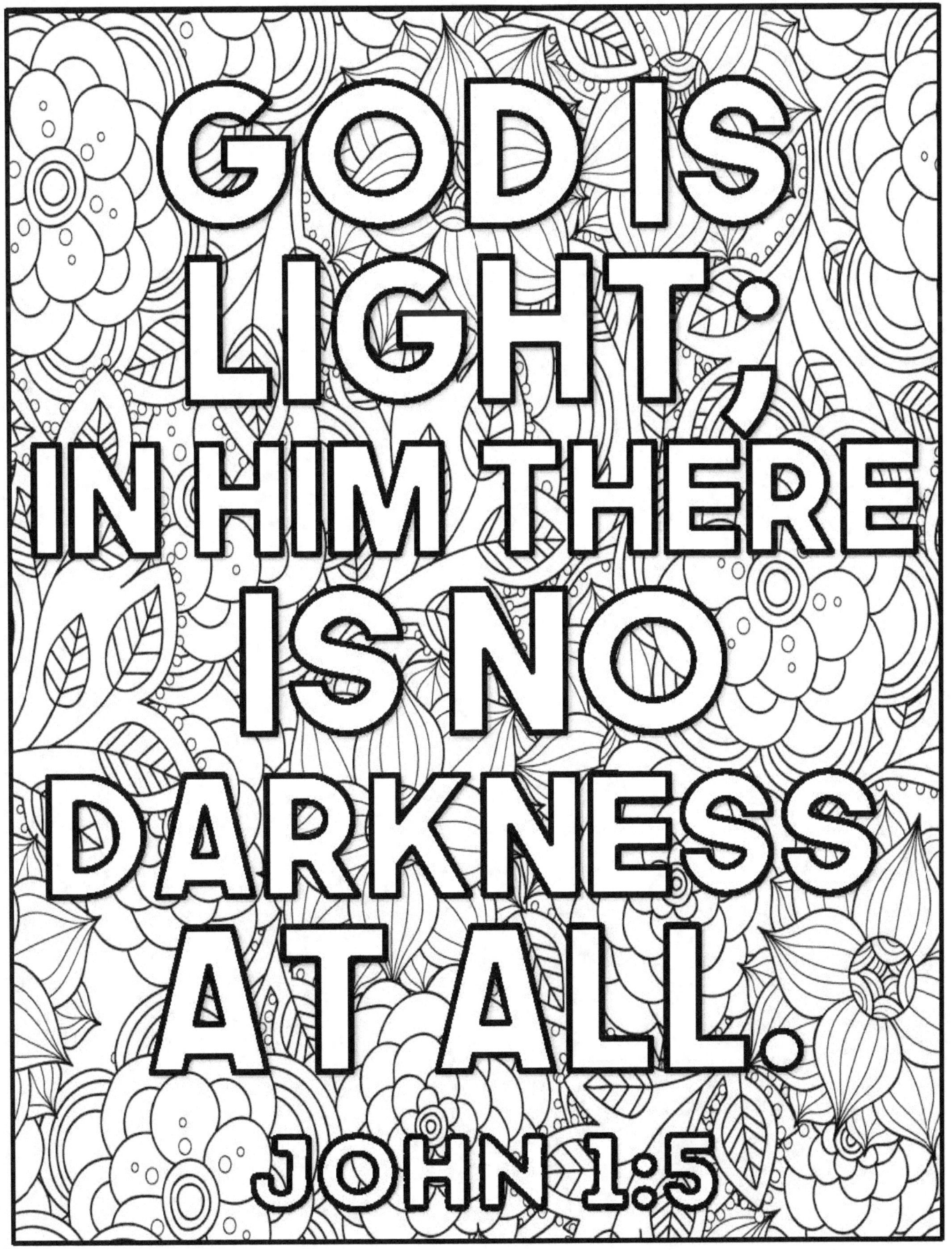

But when i am afraid, i will put my trust in you.

Psalm 56:3

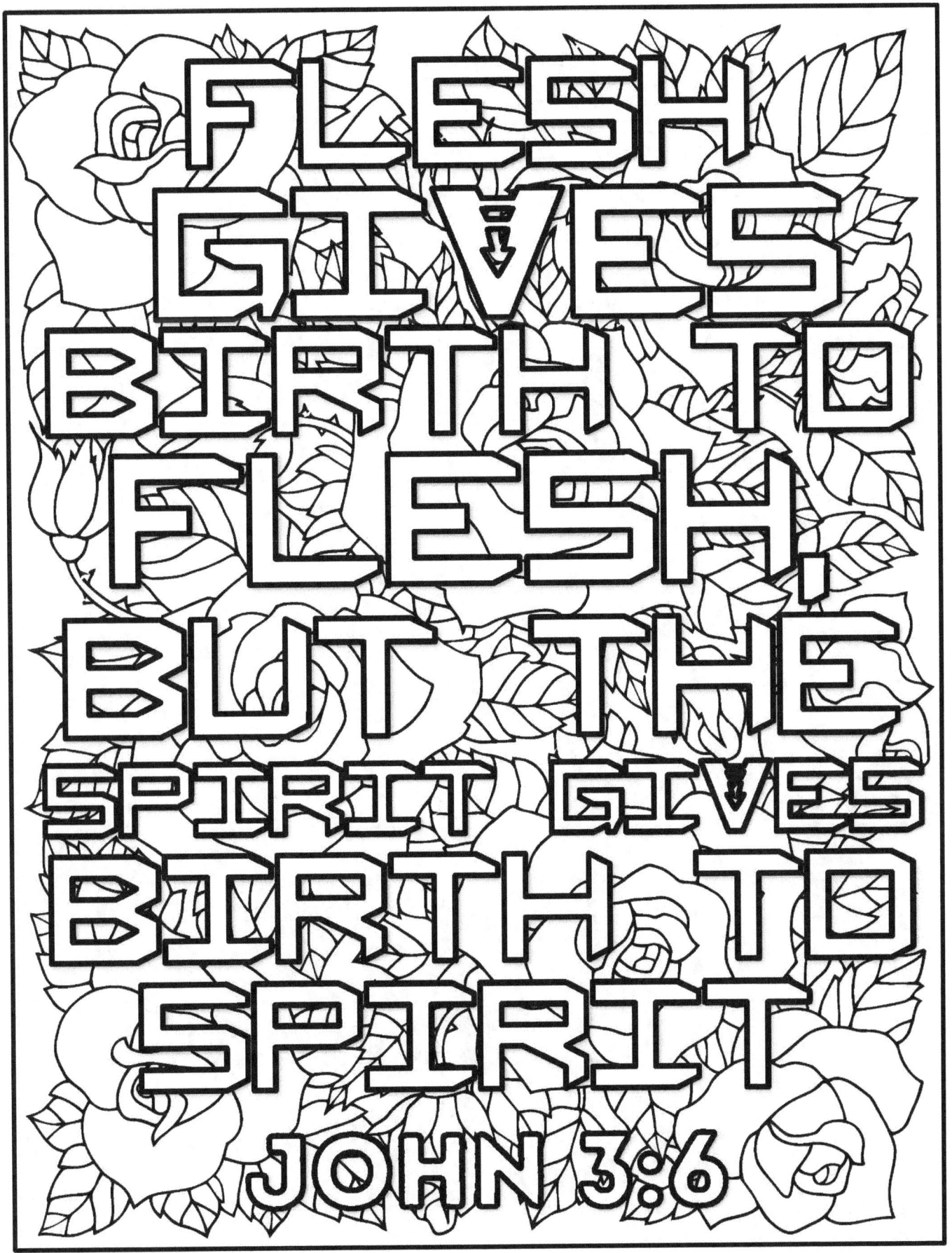

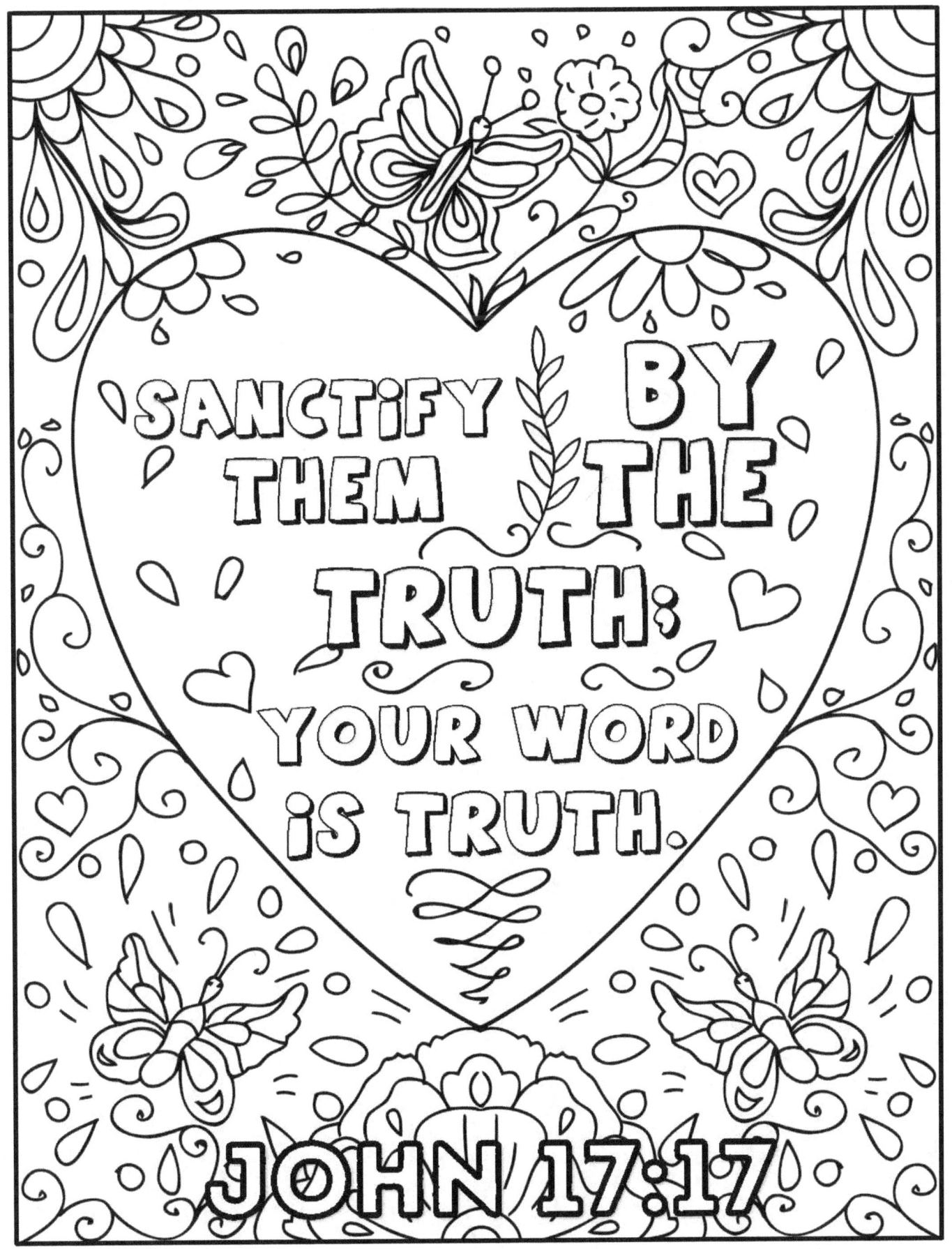

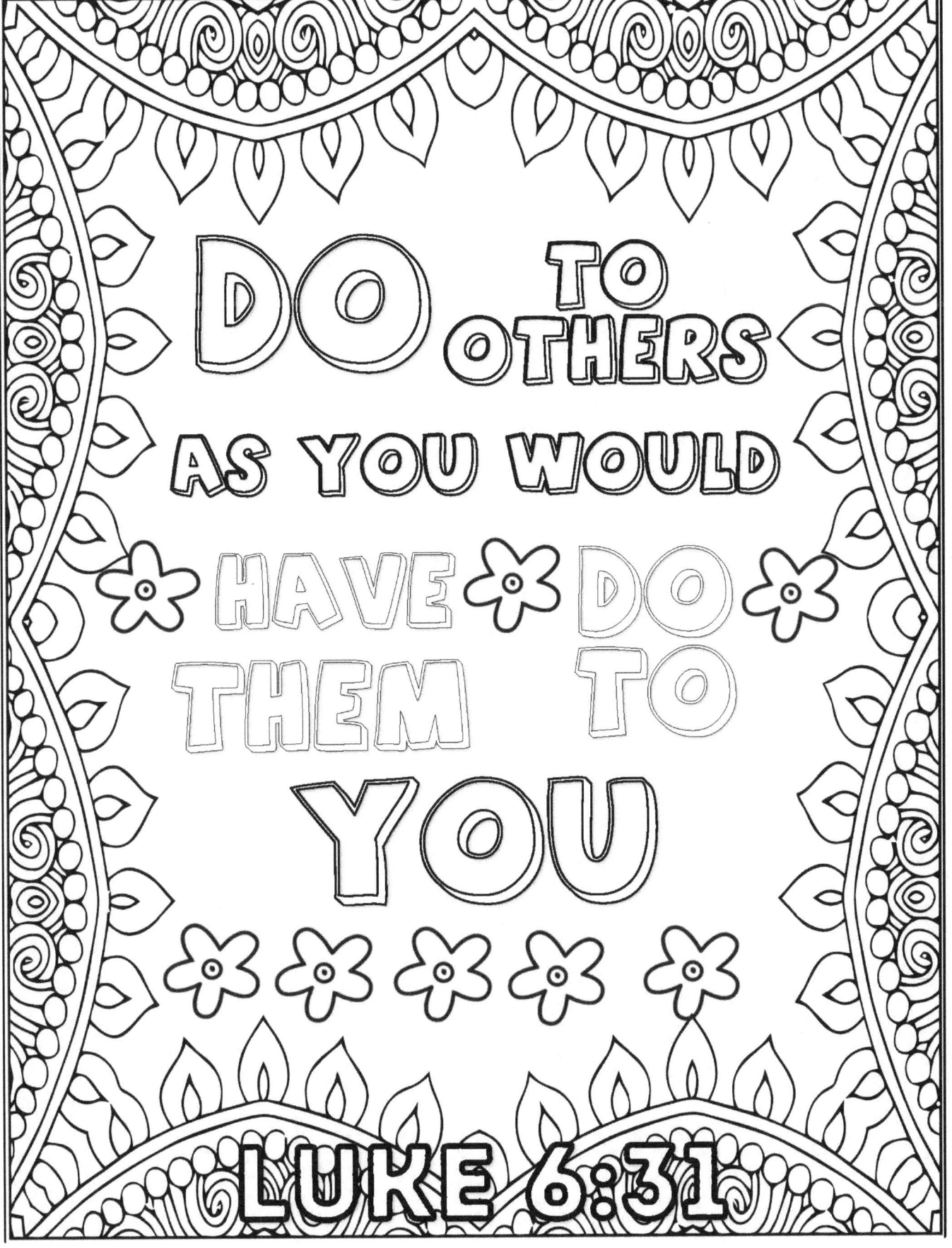

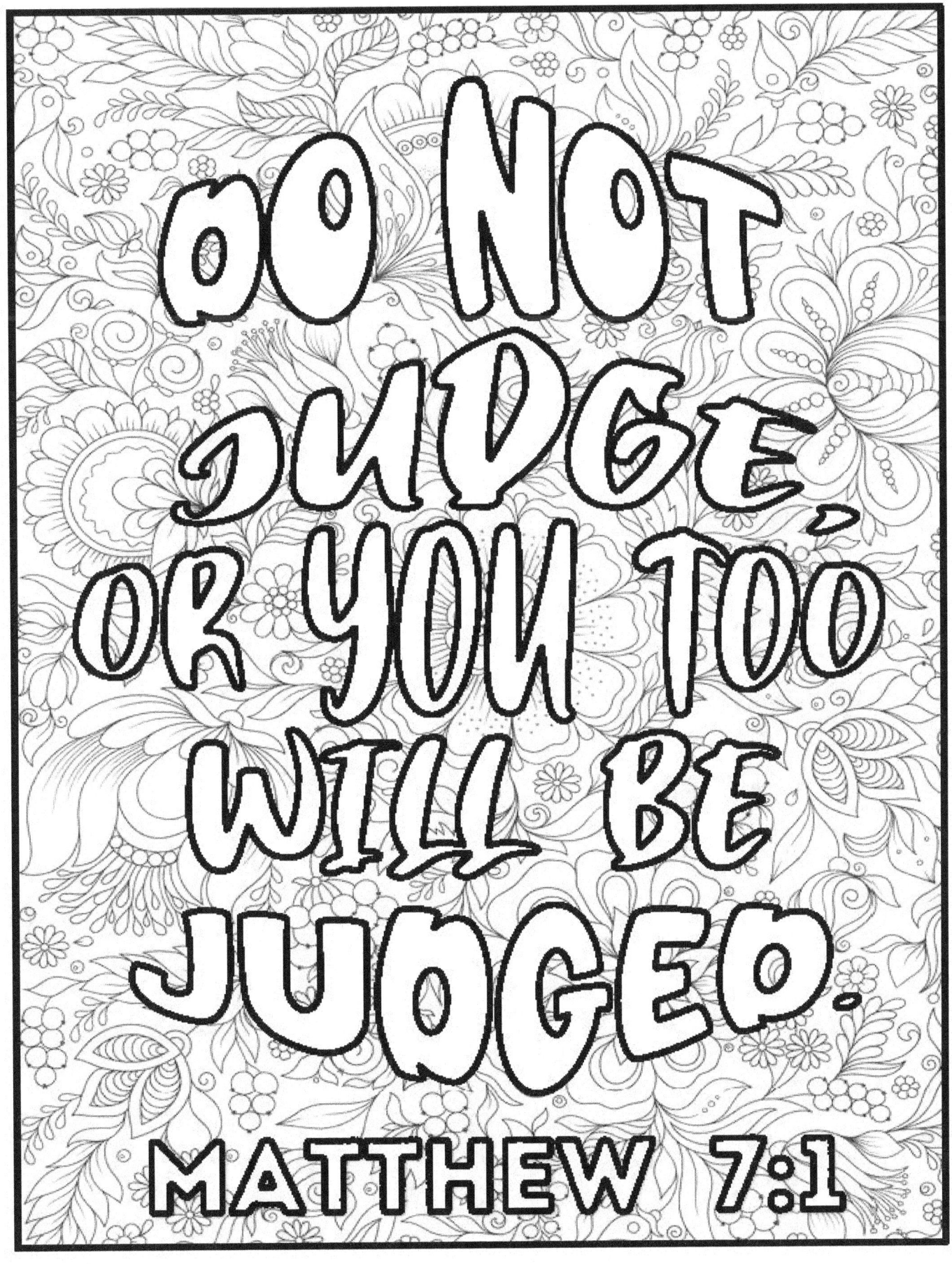

All things work together for good to those who love God and are called according to His purpose

ROMANS 8:28

About The Author

Twylia Reid is a Best-Selling-Multi-Award-Winning Author and Multi-Published non-fiction writer. Her work has appeared in numerous publications, in print, and online. 2020 Success Women National Top Influencer Nominee, 2019 Trinity Nonprofit Awards Finalist, 2019 Blacks In Government Featured Speaker, 2019 110th NAACP Conference Featured Author/Panelist Moderator, 2019 Unspoken Wounds Women Veteran's Portrait of Personal Courage Award Recipient, 2019 ACHI (Strength In Sisterhood) Magazine Woman of Achievement & Author of the Year Award Nominee, 2018 48th Congressional Legislative Caucus Featured Author, 2019 Winner of The Authors Show Health/Fitness/Wellness Top Female Author, 2018 Winner of The Authors Show Female Non-Fiction Author, The Huffington Post Expert Feature Series "Who's Who –10 Black Female Experts to Watch in 2018" selected, and 2017 American Book Fest Best Book Awards Finalist.

Minister, speaker, entrepreneur, brain-injury-community advocate and caregiver, she's the Founder of Broken Wings, Inc., a 501(c)3 non-profit organization created to assist brain injury survivors and their families, Founder of When Heaven Speaks, LLC book coaching & publishing, Founder of Broken Wings Brain Injury Empowerment Group, Warring Women Arise and Pray Group, and the Executive Producer/Host of the Conquerors Café radio show where her knowledge and expertise is used as a conduit to help empower, educate, and enlighten survivors & caregivers of traumatic events by teaching them how to create the life they desire in spite of the challenges faced after a tragedy.

Her mantra is "Aspiring to Inspire Others!" To learn more, visit her website at www.twyliareid.com.

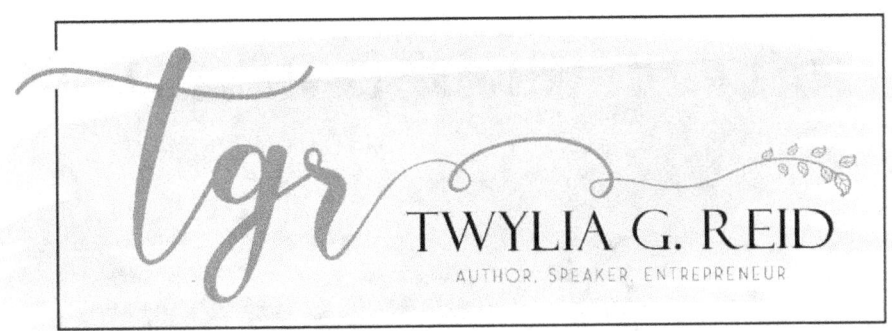

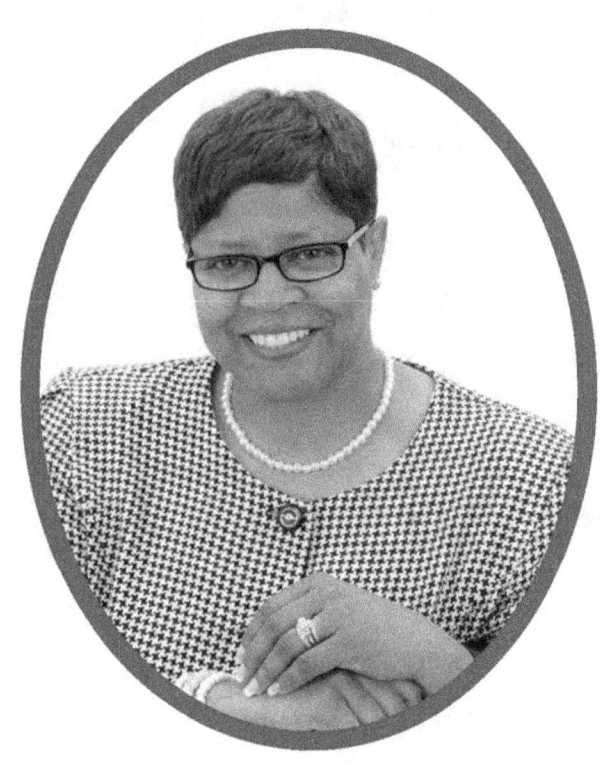

www.TwyliaReid.com
www.whenheavenspeakspublishing.com
www.brokenwingsinc.org

RECOMMENDED READINGS

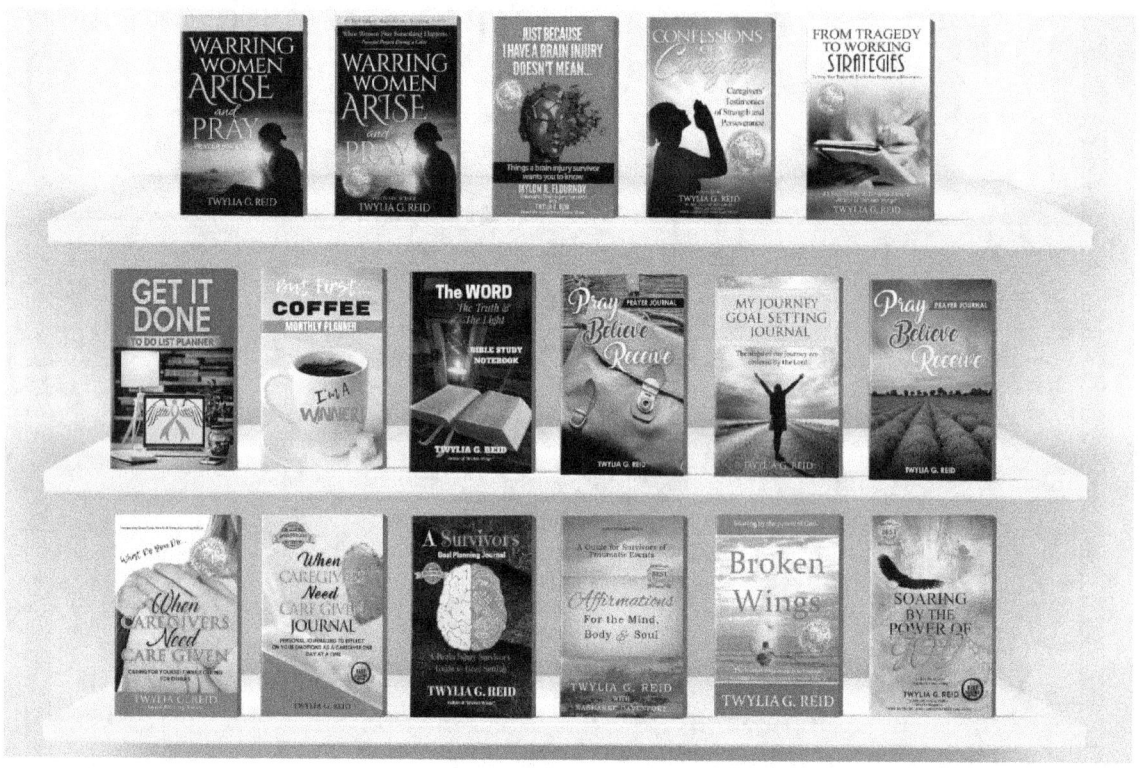

All books can be purchased from my website at
www.TwyliaReid.com
or
www.amazon.com/author/twyliareid

I pray this book is uplifting to your soul as you find peace and tranquility in the images on each page.

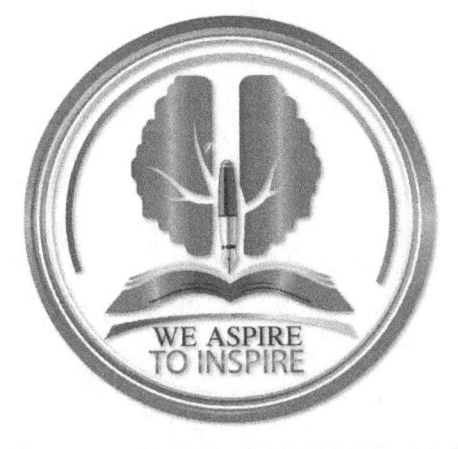

WHEN HEAVEN SPEAKS, LLC

www.whenheavenspeakspublishing.com

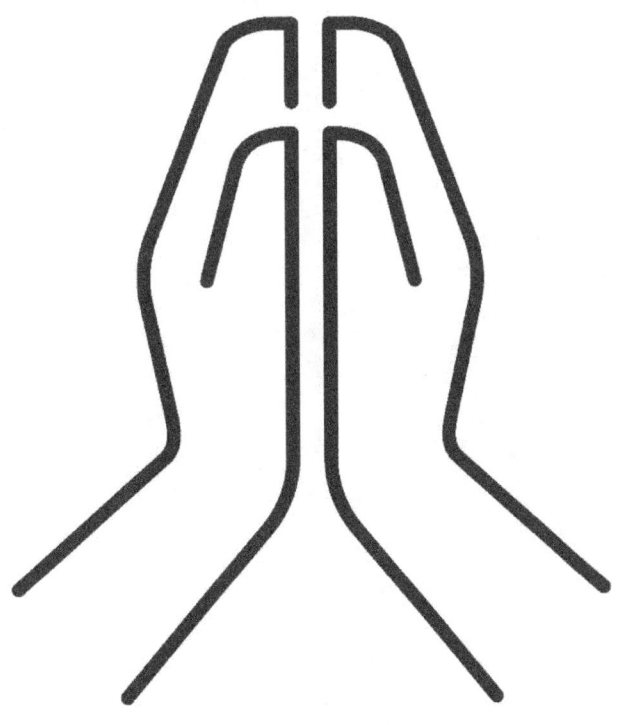

www.ingramcontent.com/pod-product-compliance
Lightning Source LLC
Chambersburg PA
CBHW082017230526
45466CB00022B/2416